EVERYD~~A~~

MADE E~~AST~~

# Ableton
# Live

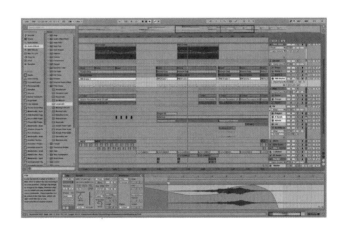

**Publisher and Creative Director:** Nick Wells
**Commisioning Editor:** Polly Prior
**Senior Project Editor:** Catherine Taylor
**Art Director & Layout:** Mike Spender
**Digital Design and Production:** Chris Herbert
**Copy Editor:** Anna Groves
**Screenshots:** Ronan Macdonald
**Proofreader:** Dawn Laker
**Indexer:** Helen Snaith

**Special thanks to:** Carolyn Bingley

This edition first published 2018 by
**FLAME TREE PUBLISHING**
6 Melbray Mews
Fulham, London SW6 3NS
United Kingdom

www.flametreepublishing.com

© 2018 Flame Tree Publishing

18 20 22 21 19
1 3 5 7 9 10 8 6 4 2

ISBN 978-1-78664-773-3

A CIP record for this book is available from the British Library upon request.

Price equivalents in brackets are rounded-down/up figures based on the exchange rate in October 2017.

Printed in China

*Everyday Gudies Made Easy: Ableton Live* is an independent publication and has not been authorized, sponsored, or
otherwise approved by Ableton AG. 'Ableton' and 'Ableton Live' and related product names are trademarks of Ableton AG.

Image Credits:
Screenshots courtesy of Ronan Macdonald and © Ableton AG, and © other relevant organizations where appropriate.
Product and lifestyle shots courtesy of and ©: **Ableton AG** 6, 7, 12, 12, 12, 14; **Focusrite Plc** 11t, 13;
**PreSonus Audio Electronics, Inc.** 11c, 119; **KRK Systems ®, Inc.** 11b; **Arturia** 47; **Zoom Corporation** 121b.
All remaining photos courtesy **Shutterstock.com** and © the following contributors: hurricanehank 3 & 108, 5;
MoonRock 8; Denis Rozhnovsky 10t; Zeynep Demir 10b; Alexandru Nika 34; Titima Ongkantong 40; Alena A 45;
lightwavemedia 54; Anutr Yossundara 56, 94; Kzenon 61; Africa Studio 73; Angelina Pilarinos 74; TippaPatt 80;
Balduk Andrey 84; DisobeyArt 87; photopixel 92; Eugenio Marongiu 106; Dundanim 110; dwphotos 114;
vectorfusionart 121 t; Luis Santos 122; Sergiy Palamarchuk 123.

EVERYDAY GUIDES
MADE EASY

# Ableton
# Live

RONAN MACDONALD

FOREWORD BY DAVE CLEWS

FLAME TREE
PUBLISHING

# CONTENTS

Before you take your first steps with Live, there are some hardware
and software accompaniments you might like to consider.

Live's Session View makes creating the compositional elements of a track easy and fun.

Learn how to use Live's powerful collection of included Audio
and MIDI effects and instruments.

Take the raw materials of your Session View exploits and refine
them into a finished track in Live's linear production interface.

Balance the tracks in your project and work them up into a professional-sounding end result.

Now that you know your way around Live, you're ready to take it out of the
studio and on to the stage, as a DJ, solo instrumentalist or band member!

# FOREWORD

**It can't be denied that the advancements made in computer technology over the last couple of decades have had an incredible effect on all of the creative arts, but perhaps none more so than in the field of music production. The rise of the Digital Audio Workstation (or DAW for short) has meant that it's never been easier to get your hands on the right set of tools for composing and arranging whatever style of music takes your fancy.**

While there are a number of these production powerhouses on the market, what makes Ableton Live unique amongst its peers is that it's been engineered not just as an application for recording, mixing and mastering music, but also, as the name suggests, for performing it in a live environment. Additional tools for beatmatching and crossfading, along with an intuitive workflow for creating mixes and arrangements on the fly, have also made it a big hit with the DJ fraternity.

So, with all of this creative power at your fingertips, all that's missing is a helping hand to get you started with the basic knowledge required to get the most out of the software – and that's exactly where this book comes in. Whether you're an absolute beginner, an intermediate user or a seasoned producer making the switch to Live from another DAW, in your hands right now is a thorough grounding in the basics of the application that will stand you in good stead for years of happy music-making to come. So let's dive in and begin your Live journey right away!

**Dave Clews**
Musician and music technology columnist

# INTRODUCTION

Ableton Live is one of the most popular DAW (digital audio workstation) applications in the world, thanks to its streamlined interface, powerful feature set and seamless merging of studio and live-performance workflows. This book gives the newcomer to Live all the knowledge and advice they need to get started.

## NEED TO KNOW

Filled with practical advice, this book is your comprehensive guide to Ableton Live. As well as showing you around the software itself, it also tells you how to get the most out of it from a creative perspective, and presents plenty of general music production tips along the way.

**Above:** Ableton Live 9.7 arrived in October 2016.

## SIX CHAPTERS

This book is divided into six chapters. The first guides you through the software and hardware you'll need to begin your Ableton Live journey. The second deals with the first phase of producing a track in Live: creating parts in the Session View. The third chapter addresses Live's library of excellent instrument and effects devices, and third-party plugins. The fourth switches to the Arrangement View, where the fruits of your Session View labours are turned into a linear tack; and chapter five tackles the mixing stage. The final chapter looks at using Live ... live, as both a DJing system and the centre of a band setup.

**Above:** Live brings new sampling features and workflows to Push.

## SMALL CHUNKS

There's a lot to cover, so each chapter is broken down into short sections, keeping everything clear and succinct, and enabling you to dip in and out as you see fit.

### Hot Tips

**Look out for Hot Tips throughout the book – bite-sized ideas and advice.**

## STEP-BY-STEP GUIDES

These walk you through a range of techniques, from quantizing MIDI and Instrument Rack construction to mix automation and cueing.

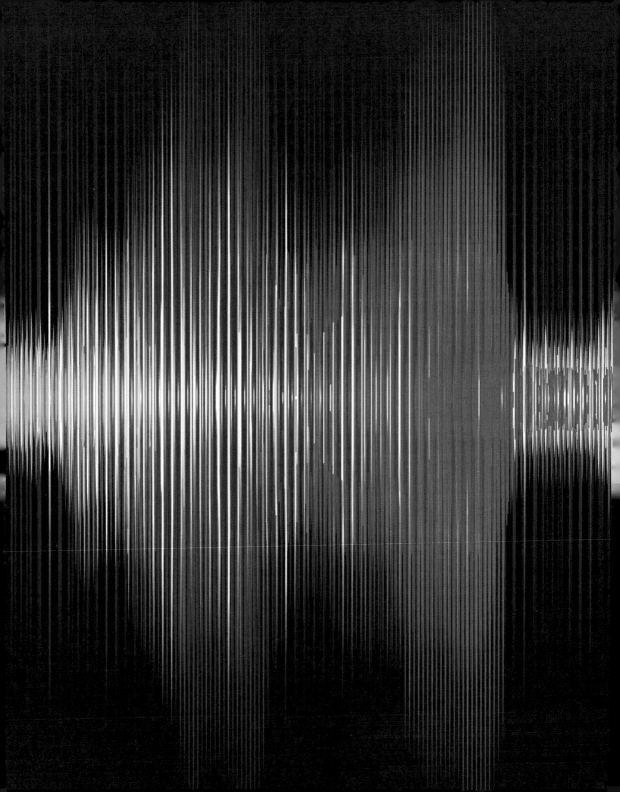

GETTING STARTED

# WHAT YOU NEED

**As well as Ableton Live and a computer on which to run it, there are a few other bits and pieces that you're going to want to acquire.**

## THE COMPUTER

You have two things to decide when buying a machine on which to run Ableton Live:

### Mac or PC?

The decision whether to go for an Apple Mac running MacOS or a PC running Windows should boil down to personal preference in terms of the physical qualities of the hardware and your familiarity and comfort with the operating system. With regard to Ableton Live itself, the software is exactly the same on either, and both run it equally well.

**Above/Below:** It doesn't matter whether you choose Mac or PC – Live works the same on both.

### Laptop or Desktop?

The answer to that will depend on how portable you want your Live rig to be. If you're looking to perform live, obviously a laptop is the only viable choice. For maximum processing power in the studio however – translating to more simultaneous virtual instruments and effects – a high-end desktop is always the better option.

# AUDIO INTERFACE AND MONITORS

Getting sound into and out of your computer is an essential consideration.

## Inputs and Outputs

While your computer's headphone output will suffice when you're starting out, eventually you're going to need a decent audio interface, especially if you're recording guitars, microphones and so on. And if you'll be DJing with Live, make sure your interface has a separately assignable headphone output for cue monitoring. Brands to look out for include those by RME, Focusrite, PreSonus, Universal Audio and Roland.

**Above**: If you're going to be recording anything from the outside world, a good audio interface is essential (Focusrite Scarlett 18i8 and PreSonus AudioBox 22VSL shown here).

## Loud and Proud

When it comes to loudspeakers, your home stereo won't really cut it, as it's designed to colour the output favourably, rather than give an honest impression of how your Live projects sound. Invest as much as you can in a pair of professional active monitors by – amongst many others – Mackie, Adam, KRK, Event or Genelec.

**Left**: Monitoring is one area where it's best to spend as much as you can (KRK VXT6 monitor shown here).

## INTRO, STANDARD OR SUITE?

There are three versions of Live available in the Ableton online shop: Intro at €79 (£70/$93), Standard at €349 (£312/$412) and Suite at €599 (£536/$707). You can see the differences between them at www.ableton.com/en/live/feature-comparison and which one you choose will come down to two things: how much you can afford of course; and how 'big' your Live projects – or Sets, to give them their proper name – are likely to get.

If you're only going to be DJing and indulging in light production work, Live Intro may well suffice. If you're looking for the full Live experience in terms of unlimited track counts and core functionality, and are planning to supplement it with third-party plugins, Standard will get you there. If, however, you want everything that Ableton has to offer, including all 10 virtual instruments, 35 audio effects, 21 Max For Live devices and 11GB of bundled sounds, Suite actually represents quite a bargain.

### Hot Tip

There is a Live Lite version that ships with some hardware controllers, such as the Akai MPK249.

**Below:** There are three Live 'tiers' – fork out for Suite if you can afford it.

# MIDI CONTROLLERS

You'll need a MIDI controller to play instruments, trigger clips and more.

## Keyboards and Pad Controllers

MIDI – that is, the note data used to play virtual instruments – is a key component of Ableton Live. While you can draw notes directly into MIDI clips, recording them in real time from a keyboard or set of drum pads is usually more conducive to an effective creative flow – particularly for the capable pianist or drummer.

**Above**: Even if you can't play keyboards, a MIDI controller is a must (Novation Launchkey 25 shown here).

There are countless MIDI controllers on the market, varying wildly in price, size, form and features, but things to look out for are: velocity sensitivity (essential): aftertouch (nice to have); hammer action (for the trained pianist); and the inclusion of assignable knobs and/or sliders for manipulating instruments, effects and the Live mixer on the fly.

## Ableton Push

Ableton offers its own dedicated Live MIDI
controller in the shape of the extraordinary
Push. This sturdily constructed 64-pad
'instrument' features dual high-res screens,
touch-sensitive knobs and a touchstrip, and is
geared up for recording and step-sequencing
drum and melodic parts, launching clips in
Session View, controlling and automating
instruments and effects, and much more.

### Hot Tip

**Although Push is unrivalled in its
command of Live, there are other
pad controllers out there that can be
set up to offer similar functionality,
including Native Instruments'
Maschine Jam, the Akai APC40 MkII
and Novation's Launchpad range.**

**Below:** For the ultimate in Live control, Push 2 is money very well spent indeed.

# PLUGINS AND SOUNDWARE

Expand Ableton Live with extra instruments, effects and sounds.

## Plugins

Ableton Live has a good number of virtual instruments and effects built in, but you can add to them whenever you like with third-party VST and (on Mac) Audio Units plugins. There are literally thousands available to buy or download for free, many of them emulating classic hardware instruments and effects, others realizing entirely new sonic concepts in spectacular style.

## Hot Tip

KVR Audio is the definitive online resource for plugin info, news and discussion – www. kvraudio.com

**Above:** Toontrack's Superior Drummer 3 plugin instrument contains six staggeringly realistic virtual drum kits.

From synthesizers and drum machines to multisampled acoustic and electric instruments of all kinds; from reverbs, compressors, EQs and delays to tape emulations, granular processors and transient shapers, plugins are central to any computer-based studio.

## Live Packs and Samples

Live comes with 4GB (Intro), 11GB (Standard) or 54GB (Suite) of sampled sounds for royalty-free use in your productions. As with plugins, an entire industry has been built around samples, with companies including Loopmasters, Time+Space, Sample Magic, Noiiz, Mode Audio and many others offering an endless array of affordable, royalty-free sampled loops and one-shots.

As the name suggests, Live Packs are bundles of samples, clips, presets and Sets put together for use with Live. A Live Pack could contain anything from a simple set of loops to a collection of full Sets, complete with multisampled instruments and Racks. Ableton themselves have an ever-expanding range of Live Packs available to buy on their website: www.ableton.com/en/packs/

**Below:** Loopmasters is one of the biggest commercial suppliers of samples in the world.

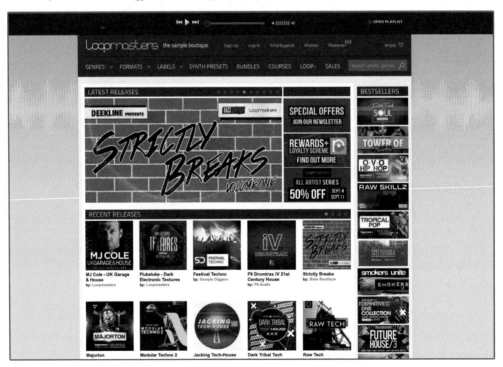

# THE LIVE INTERFACE

**Live is arguably the most easily learnt of all digital audio workstations, with its intuitive single-screen interface going out of its way to enhance rather than hamper your creative flow. Let's take a quick tour of Live and see what's what and where.**

## SESSION VIEW

Fundamental to Live's overarching concept is the Session View (above). Here, audio and MIDI clips – loops and one-off samples or 'one-shots' – are laid out in a grid and 'launched' in real time to jam out track ideas for development in the Arrangement View, and perform live. Newly launched clips wait until the start of the next bar (or other time division, as set in the Control

Bar's Quantization) to launch, and are synced to the beat using Live's warping system, so everything always stays in time.

Horizontal rows of clips are called Scenes. Clicking the play button in a Scene header on the right-hand end of the grid launches all clips on that row together.

## Hot Tip

**Flip between the Session and Arrangement Views using the two top-right buttons, or by pressing the Tab key on your keyboard.**

## ARRANGEMENT VIEW

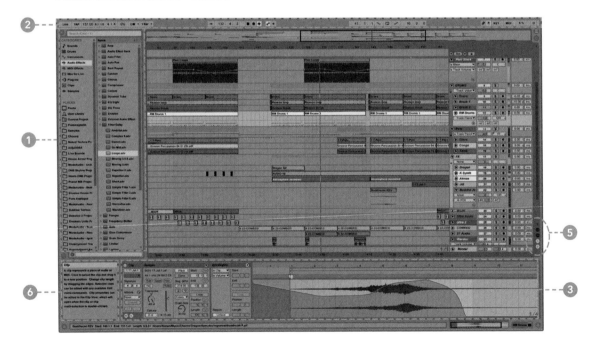

Having got the skeleton of a track together in the Session View by jamming freeform with your audio and MIDI clips, the Arrangement View (above) is where you shape it into a finished arrangement.

The Arrangement View's more 'traditional' linear interface sees the tracks in your Set running from left to right along a timeline, with a playhead progressing through them – just like a multitrack tape machine. Existing clips can be dragged, copied, added, deleted and split, new clips can be recorded directly on to tracks, and automation lanes enable mixer and device parameter movements to be captured and played back, for dynamic shaping of sounds over time.

## Hot Tip

The overview at the top lets you see the whole arrangement in miniature and set the visible area below to any range within it.

### 1 Browser

The browser makes the full contents of your Live Library and general file system available in a single pop-out panel (via the triangular button, top left) panel, with content categories and folders listed in the left-hand column and their contents navigated and selected in the right-hand column. Enter text into the Search field at the top to find the clip, plugin, preset, sample, MIDI file or other object that you're after, then once you've located it, double-click it or drag it on to the relevant track or device to load it. Click the horizontal bar with the headphones button at the bottom to audition the currently selected clip or instrument preset. With clips, the bar shows a thumbnail of the contained MIDI sequence or audio waveform.

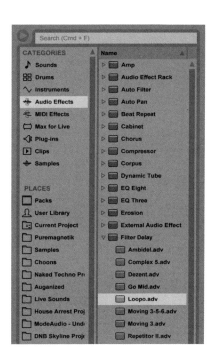

### 2 Control Bar

At the top of the interface, the Control Bar houses a range of global parameters and the transport section. At the left-hand end are the tempo controls. Set the project tempo manually by dragging up and down on the BPM field or typing directly into it, or in real time by repeatedly clicking the Tap button. Click the 'two circles' button to activate the metronome, and set the global launch Quantization (timing correction setting for triggering clips) with the right-most menu.

In the middle of the Control Bar are the transport buttons (Play, Stop and Record), playback position display, Automation Arm switch and more. The two right-hand sections handle the following: looping and record punch-in/out; activating/deactivating MIDI/automation Draw mode, Key and MIDI Map modes, and QWERTY keyboard MIDI input; and monitoring of CPU and hard-drive activity.

## ③ Detail View

The bottom of the Live interface is dominated by the Detail View, which switches between Clip and Device Views via the two long buttons, bottom right.

The Clip View contains a range of parameters for editing the currently selected clip, including an audio waveform and Warp Markers for audio clips, the MIDI Note Editor for MIDI clips, and the Clip and Envelopes boxes for both. The Device View reveals the device chain for the selected track and grants access to its constituent Racks, Instruments, MIDI and Audio Effects, and external plugins. Drag devices in from the browser and rearrange them by dragging them left and right within the chain.

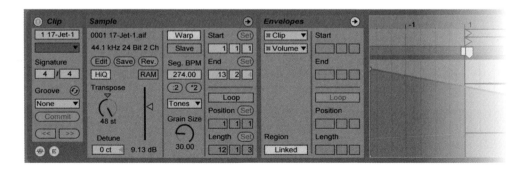

**④ Mixer (*see* page 17, Sesion View)**

Live's mixer is positioned at the bottom of the Session View and represented in simplified form at the right-hand end of the Arrangement View. It's used to blend, balance and position the tracks in your Set. The mixer essentials are all present and correct – level faders and meters, pan knobs, mute, solo and record-arm buttons, auxiliary effects send controls – and as well as the main track channels and Master output channel, up to 12 Return channels can be added for hosting auxiliary send effects.

The mixer is fully automatable and easily mapped to any MIDI controller by clicking the MIDI Map switch at the top right of the interface (keyboard shortcut: Cmd/Ctrl+M).

**⑤ Show/Hide Buttons**

Use these handy buttons to show and hide various elements of the Live interface. Specifically, these are the audio and MIDI inputs and outputs section, the device chain manager in the mixer, the auxiliary effects send controls, Return tracks, the whole mixer, the Track Delay fields (used to offset the timing of individual tracks) and the Crossfader section.

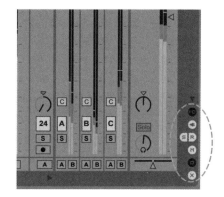

**⑥ Info View**

Live's manual is excellent, but when you need to know in a hurry what a certain control or interface element does, the Info View gives a summary of whatever's under the mouse pointer. Press Shift+? to open and close it. As well as the help text, you can enter your own info for individual tracks, devices and clips – simply right-click and look for the 'Edit Info Text' option in the pop-up menu.

> **Device**
>
> Click in a device's title bar to select it. Devices can be dragged to new positions within the device chain, or to new tracks in the Session or Arrangement Views. Dragging a device to its folder in the Device Browser saves its current settings as a preset.

CREATING A TRACK

# THE SESSION VIEW

It may look like a spreadsheet, but Live's Session View is a powerful creative environment for experimenting with compositional ideas and piecing together sections of a track. Here, we're going to talk about tracks, clips and scenes.

## ADDING TRACKS

Live is capable of running as many audio and MIDI tracks as your Mac or PC can handle. In the Session View, tracks appear as vertical columns of clip slots, and there are five track types: Audio, MIDI, Return (for hosting send effects), Master (the final output channel, of which there can only ever be one) and Group (combining multiple tracks for collective mixing and processing).

**Below:** Head to the Create menu to insert new tracks.

To make a new Audio, MIDI or Return track in the Session (and, indeed, Arrangement) View, select the relevant Insert options from the Create menu. To make a Group Track, select the individual tracks you want it to contain and choose Group Track from the Edit menu (Command/Ctrl+G). To rename the track from its default 'Audio', 'MIDI', etc., select Edit > Rename (Cmd/Ctrl+R).

# CLIP SLOTS

The stacked 'cells' in each Audio or MIDI track are called clip slots, and each one holds a clip of that track type, either recorded or imported, for triggered playback. By experimenting with different combinations of clips across multiple tracks – variations on a bassline on one, variations on a drum loop on the next, and so on – you can build up ideas for a song or create a dynamic live performance.

## Hot Tip

**To change the colour of a clip or track, right-click it and pick a hue from the palette at the bottom.**

A loaded clip slot displays the name of the clip (rename it with Cmd/Ctrl+R), and a triangular play button. Clips are moved between clip slots by dragging, and copied by Option+dragging. An empty clip slot contains just a square stop button, for stopping playback of any clip on that track.

**Below**: Change the width of Session View tracks by dragging the right-hand edges of their title bars.

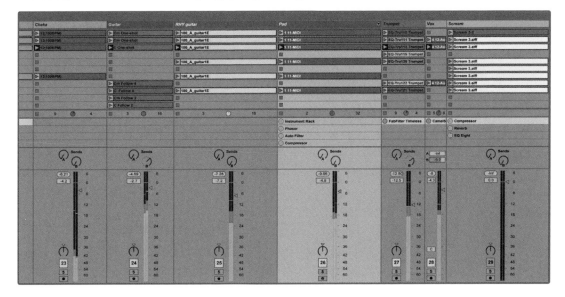

## Launching Clips

Launch a clip in any clip slot by clicking its triangular play button. (Your live Set will start playing if it isn't already.) The button will flash green and playback won't actually start until the next time division set in the Control Bar Quantization menu (1 Bar by default) is reached, making it impossible to trigger clips out of time with each other (assuming they're correctly prepared and warped in the first place, which we'll come to later). Only one clip can play back on a track – launching a second stops the first.

To stop playback of a clip, click the square stop button in any empty slot or at the bottom of the track.

At the bottom of each track is a progress indicator, visualizing playback of the currently playing clip. If the clip is set to Loop mode, the indicator is an endlessly cycling wheel. If not, it's a 'one-shot' horizontal bar.

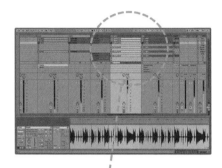

**Below**: Looping clips have cycling progress indicators, while one-shots are displayed horizontally.

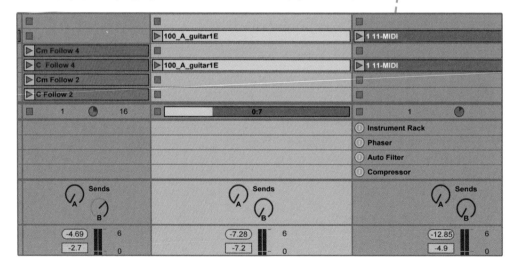

# LOADING DEVICES

1. Live's built-in virtual instruments and effects – collectively called devices – are loaded on to MIDI, Audio, Group and Return tracks, and the Master track, by dragging them on to the track itself or into its Detail View.

2. MIDI tracks can host MIDI Effects, Instruments and Audio Effects. MIDI Effects transform the MIDI data coming in from the clips on the track in various ways, before routing it to the loaded instrument. The output of the instrument is then processed using Audio Effects.

**Below**: This Instrument track is hosting a MIDI Effect, an Instrument and two Audio Effects.

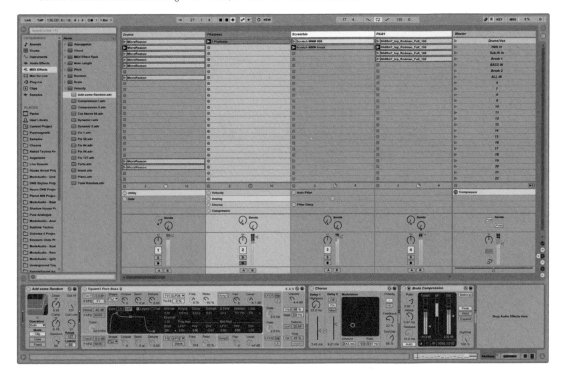

3.  Audio tracks, Return tracks and the Master track can only hold Audio Effects. On an Audio track, these process the currently playing audio clip. On a Return track, they process the signals sent to them via any track's Send controls. On the Master track, Audio Effects process every sound in the Set.

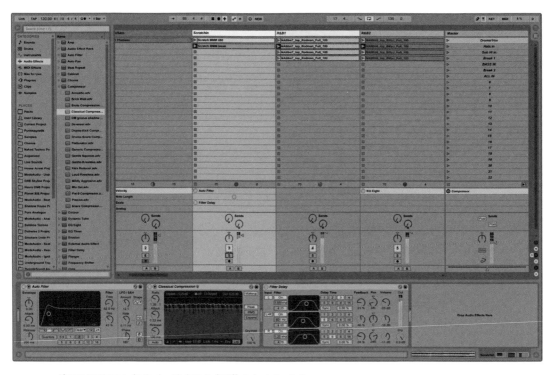

**Above:** Here's an Audio Track, with three Audio Effects loaded on to it.

# SCENES AND THE MASTER TRACK

A Scene is a horizontal row of clips, all of which are triggered at once when the Scene Launch button is clicked in the Master track. The idea, then, is to build up a song by creating Scenes containing the parts required for each section – verse, chorus, bridge, etc. – then simply step through them to 'perform' the song and record it into the Arrangement View. Like clips, Scenes adhere to the Quantization setting for perfect launch timing, so you can launch a Scene while another is playing at any point in the bar, safe in the knowledge that the switch from one to the other won't happen until the next downbeat.

## Hot Tip

**You can embed a time signature and/or tempo change into a Scene by appending its name with '3/4', '5/4', etc., and/or 'X BPM', where 'X' is the new tempo.**

Clips can be freely triggered and combined across all the tracks in your Set, and when you hit upon a combination you like – for the chorus, say – you can save it as a Scene by selecting Create > Capture and Insert Scene (Cmd/Ctrl+Shift+I).

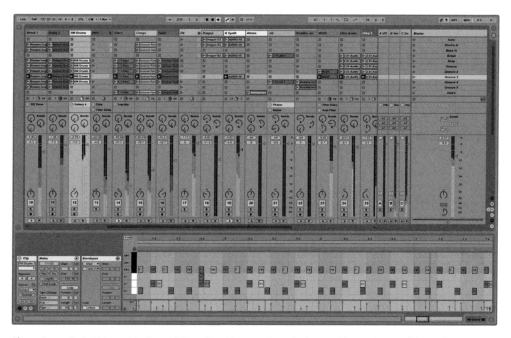

**Above:** Here, we've just triggered the Groove 3 Scene, launching every clip on that horizontal layer at the start of the next bar.

The Master track doesn't hold any clips – it's a mixer channel to which all the other tracks are ultimately routed for forwarding to your audio interface and, ultimately, monitor speakers. It has a volume fader, a pan dial and a cue control, which we'll come back to later (see page 113).

# THE CLIP VIEW

Double-clicking an Audio or MIDI clip opens it in the Clip View. Here's what you'll find there:

### Zooming, Scrolling and Selecting

1.  The Clip View shows the entirety of the selected clip and lets you edit its contents. To zoom in, place the mouse pointer above the timeline (it'll turn into a magnifying glass), then click and drag down to zoom in and up to zoom out. Double-click to reset to fully zoomed-out.

**Above:** Here's the Clip View showing the waveform for the selected audio clip.

2.  To scroll left and right through the zoomed-in clip, click and drag the magnifying glass left and right.

3.  If the zoomed-in clip is the one currently playing on its track, you can set it to scroll so that the playhead is always onscreen by clicking the Follow button in the Control Bar (Cmd/Ctrl+Shift+F).

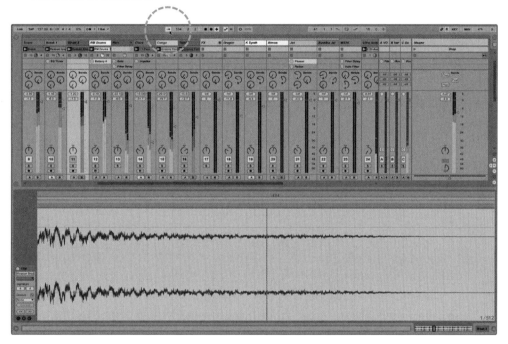

**Above:** And here's the same Clip View waveform again, now zoomed in. Click the Follow button to see the clip scroll automatically.

## Region and Loop Controls

1.  Every clip contains Start and End markers for defining the region within it to be played back (the whole thing by default). They're the bottom two triangular handles at either end of the timeline – playback begins at the Start marker when the clip is launched, and stops when it reaches the End marker.

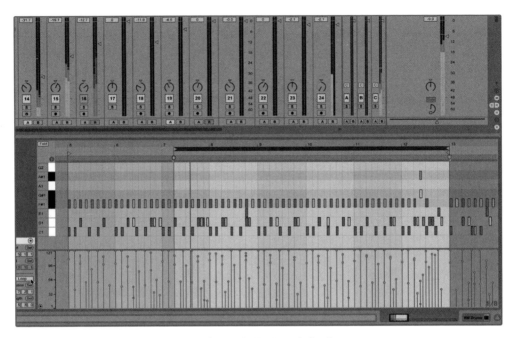

**Above:** The solid black bar at the top of the highlighted area in the Clip View is the loop brace.

2.   The top two triangular markers define the start and end points of a second region within
     the clip that cycles continuously when the Loop button is engaged in the Clip View's Notes
     or Sample box. Playback starts at the clip Start marker and jumps back to the Loop Start
     marker when the playhead reaches the Loop End marker. The loop range is represented by
     the thick beam connecting the two Loop markers – the 'loop brace'.

## Clip and Launch Boxes

At the left-hand end of the Clip View, hidden and revealed using the tiny buttons below them,
are the four clip property boxes: Clip (always present), Launch, Sample/Notes and Envelope. With
these, a wide range of parameters can be adjusted for the selected clip. The Clip box has fields
for setting the name, colour and displayed time signature of the clip, applying a groove from the
Groove Pool, and nudging playback backwards and forwards by the launch Quantization value.

In the Launch box, Launch Mode determines how clip playback stops in relation to mouse/MIDI input – you'll want to leave it at Trigger the vast majority of the time. Below that, the Quantization menu enables launch timing offset for the selected clip to be set independently of the global launch Quantization setting in the Control Bar, or turned off altogether for instant playback when launched. The Velocity field sets the amount by which the velocity of MIDI notes used to launch clips affects their volume level (via the MIDI Map option: press Cmd/Ctrl+M, select a clip slot and hit a key/pad on your MIDI controller to assign). At the default 0%, clips play back at full volume no matter what; at 100%, low-velocity MIDI notes result in very quiet playback.

The Legato button sets playback of the clip to start at the point on the timeline at which a previously playing, overlapped clip is cut off. We'll come back to Follow Actions, and the Sample/Notes and Envelopes boxes later.

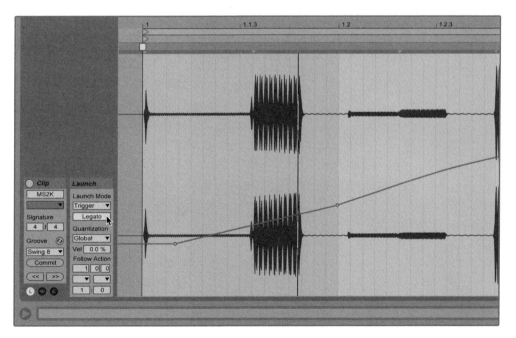

**Above:** You'll find the Clip and Launch boxes at the left-hand end of the Clip View.

# WORKING WITH AUDIO CLIPS

Way back in 2001, the very first version of Live revolutionized the timestretching and manipulation of audio thanks to Ableton's groundbreaking warping engine. With Live 9, there's practically nothing you can't do with your sampled loops, one-shots and recordings.

## WHAT IS AUDIO?

First, a quick explanation is in order.

### Audio and Audio Clips Explained

A digital audio file – also known as a sample – is a representation of a real-world sound, captured via a microphone or direct input into an audio interface. In principle, it's exactly the same thing as a recording made to tape, but with several obvious advantages, including almost no physical storage requirement, no degradation over time and random access playback.

An audio clip in Live is a visible and editable region in the Session or Arrangement View that references a sample/recording stored on your hard drive. Playing back the clip plays back the sample – or the region of it that the clip has been cut or resized to cover. The clip also contains data governing many aspects of playback, including Warp Markers, pitch, volume and parameter automation.

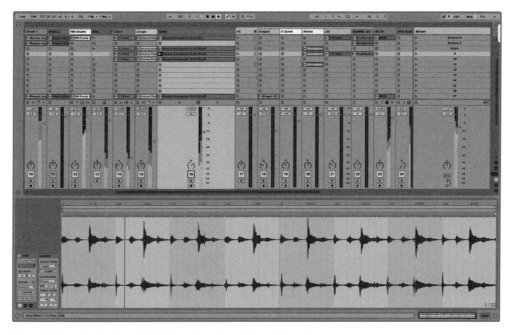

**Above**: With an audio clip selected, the Clip View shows the waveform of the sample it contains.

# IMPORTING AND RECORDING AUDIO

There are two ways to get audio into Live: record it yourself or import it from your hard drive.

## Importing Audio

Samples are imported into Live in either of two ways. The first is by dragging audio files into clip slots or Arrangement View tracks from the MacOS Finder or Windows Explorer.

The second is to drag them in from the browser, where those included in the Live Library appear in the Samples category. Any folder on your hard drive (including the drive itself) can be placed in the sidebar by clicking the Add Folder button at the bottom.

Upon import, the file appears as a clip in the Session View Slot or Arrangement View track into which it was dragged, and an Analysis file (*.asd) containing warp data, a waveform overview and other properties is created alongside the file in its folder.

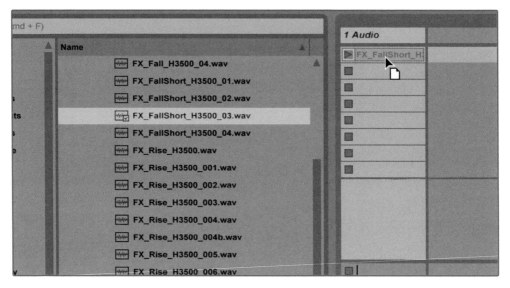

**Above:** Drag a sample from the browser into a clip slot to load it as an audio clip.

## Preparing to Record Audio

Recording audio directly into the Session View involves a few preparatory steps. The first is to set your audio interface as the Audio Input Device in Live's Preferences, and select the input(s) to which your source instrument(s) or microphone(s) is/are connected in the Audio From menu, found in the mixer's in/out section on the track to which you want to record. (This section is shown/hidden using the tiny I-O button to the right of the Master channel.)

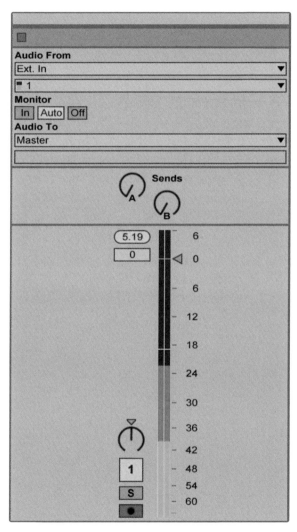

**Above:** This audio track is all set for monitoring and recording.

Your audio interface probably features direct monitoring, enabling you to feed incoming audio straight to your speakers/headphones. To monitor through Live (so you can process the sound with Live's effects in real time), you'll need to set Monitor on the target track(s) to On or Auto. Auto activates monitoring only when the track is armed for recording.

The final step is to record arm the track(s) by clicking the 'black dot' button at the very bottom of the channel strip.

## Recording Audio

With your target track(s) armed for recording, activate the metronome in the Control Bar and/or start playback of your Set, then click the Record button(s) in one or multiple clip slots to start recording into it/ them at the next time division set in the Quantization menu – 1 Bar by default.

If you initiate recording without starting playback first, you'll get a count-in, the length of which is set in the menu next to the metronome, after which playback of the Set and recording into the clip slots will both begin.

The Record buttons in the activated clip slots turn to red Launch buttons to indicate that they're currently recording. When you're done, click the Launch button(s) again to have recording stop and playback of the recorded clip(s) start seamlessly at the next Quantization note value. Your recorded samples are stored in the Set's Samples/Recorded folder. You can also record into the Arrangement View, but we'll get to that later (*see* page 84).

**Hot Tip**

**To start recording on all armed clip slots in the current Scene, click the Session Record button in the Control Bar. Click the adjacent New button while recording to stop recording at the next Quantization value and advance selection to the next Scene, creating a new one if one doesn't already exist.**

**Below:** Here, we're recording into the clip slots in Scene 2 on Tracks 1 and 2.

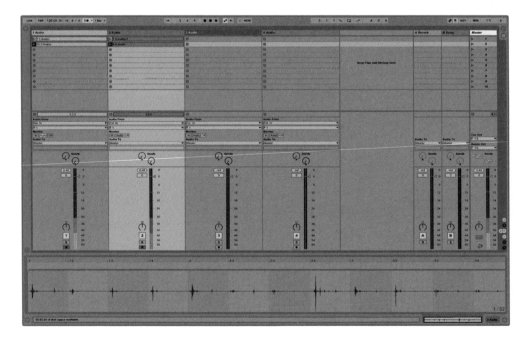

# WARPING AUDIO

Live's warping engine automatically timestretches audio clips to keep them in sync through project tempo changes, and lets you pull their internal timing around to fix and transform them.

## Warping Controls, Warp Modes and Looping

Depending on the Warp settings in Live's Preferences, audio clips may or may not warp automatically upon import. To manually activate and deactivate warping, click the Warp button in the Sample box of the Clip View. Live analyses the file to ascertain its tempo – it might get this wrong by a factor of 2 or 0.5, in which case click the Seg. BPM :2 or *2 buttons to correct. Having been warped (and possibly had a few Warp Markers moved around – *see* below), an audio clip will always stay in time with the project tempo, and, consequently, all other warped clips.

**Below:** This section of a drum track has been warped in Beats mode and looped – the original recording was at 88bpm, but it automatically plays back at our project tempo of 98bpm.

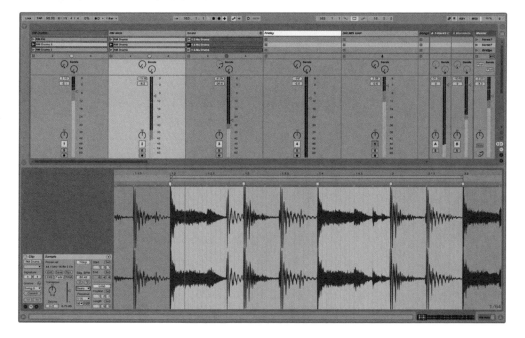

Six warp modes offer a range of granular resynthesis algorithms, each suited to a different type of source material, five of them allowing adjustment of one or two salient parameters. Beats, for example, is the best fit for drums and other transient-heavy sounds, with its Preserve and Transient Loop Mode controls letting you tailor the algorithm to optimize the all-important transient integrity. Tones is ideal for vocals and monophonic instruments; Texture is for polyphonic

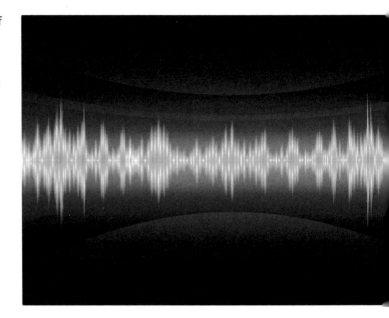

material (strings, pads, etc.); Re-Pitch works like a turntable or tape, raising/lowering the pitch as the tempo Is increased/decreased; and Complex and Complex Pro are intensive algorithms intended for use on complicated polyphonic sources and full tracks.

Activate the Loop button to the right to switch a warped audio clip from one-shot to looping mode, cycling playback when launched until manually stopped.

## Creating and Adjusting Warp Markers

If your imported audio clip is relatively even in its timing and one, two, four or eight bars long (or a full track – see page 110), Live will usually warp it correctly. If it doesn't, though, you can fix it by creating and moving Warp Markers within it.

A Warp Marker is a movable handle in the Sample Editor that 'pins' the audio at that point to the timeline. When you first import a sample, Live analyses it and marks detected transients (drum hits, for example) with small triangles above the waveform. Moving the mouse pointer over these triangles reveals temporary Warp Markers. Dragging a temporary Warp Marker with no regular Warp Markers to its right timestretches the whole clip up to the next regular Warp Marker to the left.

Double-clicking a temporary Warp Marker or any point in the Sample Editor creates a regular Warp Marker. Dragging a regular Warp Marker left and right moves that point forwards and backwards in time, timestretching the audio on both sides up to the neighbouring Warp

## Hot Tip

To instantly snap all Warp Markers in a clip exactly to the timing grid, right-click the Sample Editor and select Quantize (Cmd/Ctrl+U).

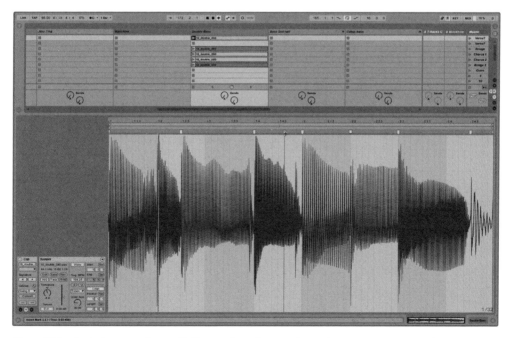

**Above:** This bassline has been manually warped in Tones mode – we've snapped its attack transients to precise note values.

Markers, which stay locked in place. Thus, discrete sections of audio can be timestretched without affecting the rest of the clip. Warp Markers snap to the grid, allowing you to effortlessly lock, for example, the snare in a drum loop exactly to the backbeat. The new tempo of each stretched section is shown in the Warp box's Seg. BPM field.

## THE SAMPLE BOX

As well as the Warp controls, the Clip View's Sample box also contains an assortment of parameters for the audio clip as a whole. These include Clip Gain (volume) and Transpose (up to four octaves of pitchshifting up or down, with optional High Quality mode), applying 4-ms fades to the start and end to reduce clicks, Sample Reverse and more.

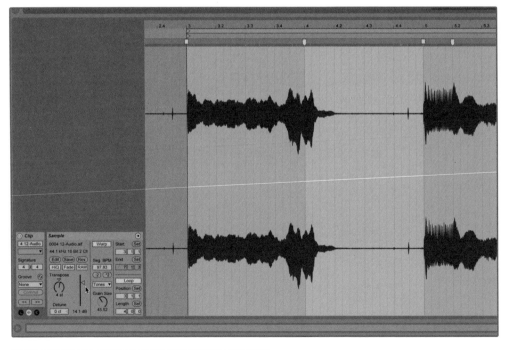

**Above:** Make top-level adjustments to your audio clips in the Sample box.

# AUDIO CLIP AUTOMATION

Draw or record real-time clip, device and mixer parameter adjustments directly into the Clip View to bring dynamism and movement to your tracks.

## Clip Envelopes

1. Select the Clip View's Envelopes box (revealed and hidden with the E button under the Clip box) and choose a parameter for automation in its Device and Control Chooser menus. These include mixer Volume, Pan and Sends, Transposition, Sample Offset and every control on every device loaded on to the clip's track.

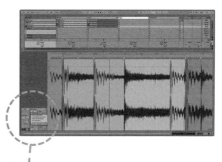

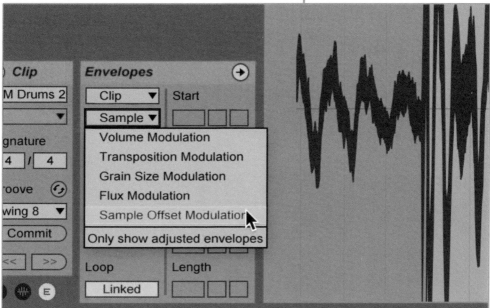

**Above**: Step1: Various sample properties can be automated using Clip Envelopes.

2. Click the red line overlaid on top of the waveform to add a few breakpoints, then drag them into position to shape your automation envelope, which will move the parameter accordingly as the clip plays. Hold the Option key and drag up and down on the line between two breakpoints to bend it into a curve.

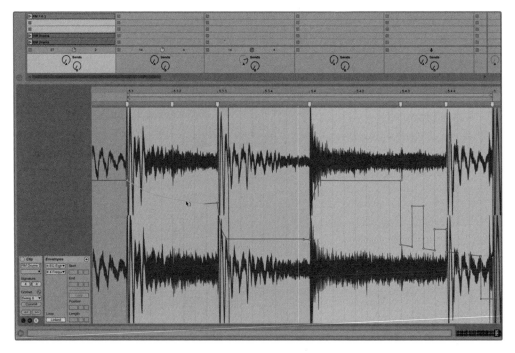

**Above:** Step 3: Automate a filter sweep using the EQ Eight tool.

3. To draw a 'step sequence' in the curve, press the B key to switch to the pencil tool (repeat to switch back) and click anywhere in the waveform. The height at which you click determines the value of the step, and the current Grid setting (narrowed and widened in the Options menu) determines its width. Here, we've automated a filter sweep using Live's EQ Eight. Parameter movements made while recording are captured as automation too.

# WORKING WITH MIDI CLIPS

**Used for triggering plugin instruments and external synths, MIDI is at the heart of Ableton Live's versatile compositional workflow.**

## WHAT IS MIDI?

Short for Musical Instrument Digital Interface, MIDI is the industry standard protocol for triggering and controlling synthesizers, samplers and other devices, both real and virtual.

### MIDI and MIDI Clips Explained

While an audio clip is a perfect digital representation of a recorded sound, a MIDI clip contains the notes and other parameters used to trigger virtual instruments within Live, as well as real-world synths and samplers connected via a MIDI interface and routed to using the MIDI track's MIDI To menu.

A MIDI clip appears in the Clip View as a series of rectangular note 'bars' laid out in a piano-roll sequencer with the keyboard on the vertical axis and the timeline on the horizontal axis. The vertical position of a note, therefore, determines its pitch, while the length determines its duration.

Notes are entered by recording or drawing with Live's pencil tool, and edited by dragging and resizing. MIDI clips also contain Velocity messages, defining the volume of each note, amongst other things, as well as other data for automating instrument parameters.

**Below:** This MIDI clip contains a piano part, recorded via a MIDI keyboard.

# RECORDING AND IMPORTING MIDI CLIPS

There are two ways to get MIDI clips into your Live Set: recording in real time or importing from the browser.

## Assigning a MIDI Keyboard

To record your own MIDI clips, you're going to need a MIDI keyboard or pad controller. Assuming you have either (or both!) connected to your computer,

## Hot Tip

When you don't have a MIDI keyboard to hand, activate the little keyboard button at the right-hand end of the Control Bar to use the top two rows of your computer's QWERTY keyboard for note input. The Z and X keys shift the octave range, while C and V decrease and increase velocity.

**Below:** Record MIDI clips directly into Live from your MIDI keyboard (such as the Arturia MiniLab mkII).

make sure its Track and Remote inputs are turned on in Live's MIDI Preferences page, and that the target track's MIDI From field is set to either All Ins or the keyboard/controller itself.

## Importing and Recording

MIDI clips are created via the same processes as audio clips. To import a MIDI file, drag it in from the browser or file system. To record your MIDI keyboard, set the Monitor section of the destination track to On or Auto for auditioning; arm the track for recording; activate the metronome (or not); start playback of the Set (or not) and click the Record button in the target clip slot. Recording will start at the next time division set in the launch Quantization menu and continue until you click the clip's Launch button or stop playback.

### Hot Tip

To add notes to an existing MIDI clip without overwriting it, select the clip and click the Session Record button in the transport controls.

**Below:** Live makes recording and overdubbing MIDI easy.

To draw a MIDI clip by hand, double-click a clip slot to create the clip, then use the pencil (invoked with the B key) and pointer tools to draw, delete, move and resize (drag the left- and right-hand ends) notes within it.

## Audio to MIDI

Live's Audio to MIDI function 'converts' audio clips to MIDI clips by extracting timing and pitch data from them and turning the results into notes on the piano roll. Use it to capture the rhythm, melody and feel of an audio recording as a MIDI sequence, keep MIDI parts in key with accompanying audio parts, and figure out chords.

There are four Audio to MIDI modes available in an audio clip's right-click menu. Slice to New MIDI Track slices the clip at its detected transients or one of a variety of beat divisions, places each audio slice on a pad in a Drum Rack and creates a MIDI clip on a new MIDI track containing the note sequence required to trigger the slices exactly as originally heard – simply edit the notes to re-sequence the part.

The other three modes – Convert Harmony/Melody/ Drums to New MIDI Track – are designed for polyphonic, monophonic and drum kit recordings respectively, each extracting the MIDI note data to a MIDI clip on a new track loaded with a sampled piano, synth or drum kit instrument. Afterwards, you can change the instrument to one of your own choosing and reshape the part by editing the MIDI notes.

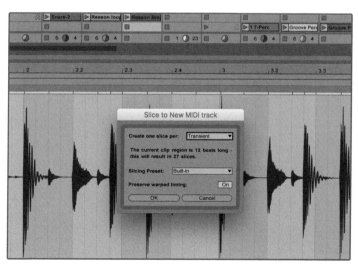

**Above**: The Slice to New MIDI Track command turns any audio clip into a Drum Rack.

# EDITING MIDI CLIPS

MIDI clips are even more flexible than audio clips in terms of editing.

### Working in the Piano Roll

Selecting a MIDI clip calls it up in the Clip View as notes in a piano-roll editor, with the Velocity Editor underneath. The vertical position of each note determines its pitch, horizontal placement represents its trigger point on the timeline, length defines its duration, and the height of the 'lollipop' in the Velocity Editor sets its velocity from 1–127.

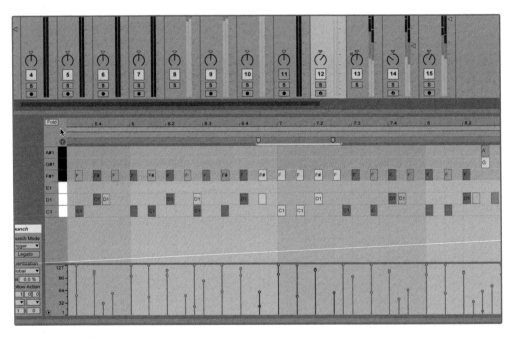

**Above:** Click the Fold button to only see the note pitches you're using – great for programming drums.

Notes can be selected and edited individually or in groups. Move them with the mouse or cursor keys, with or without snapping them to the grid, as controlled in the Options menu; and add new notes by double-clicking with the pointer tool or single-clicking with the pencil tool (B). Click the headphones button above the keyboard to preview the sound source every time a note is adjusted, and the Fold button to filter the visible note pitches to only those used.

## MIDI QUANTIZE

1. Applying quantize instantly snaps the selected notes to the Quantize grid, or all of them if none are selected. To access the Quantize settings, press Cmd/Ctrl+ Shift+U or choose it in the MIDI Note Editor right-click menu.

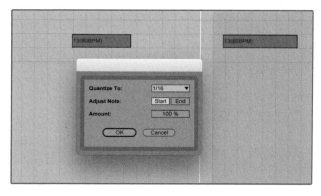

**Above:** Step 1: Snap the start and end of selected notes with Quantize.

2. The Quantize settings dialogue box lets you change the resolution of the Quantize grid, decide whether to snap the start and/or end of each note to it, and tweak the percentage amount by which notes are moved towards the grid lines.

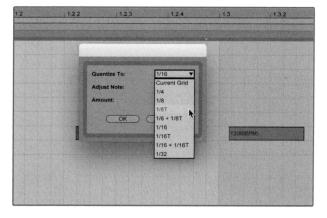

**Above:** Step 2: Set your Quantize to a musical note value.

3.  Clicking Okay in the Quantize settings dialogue box quantizes the selected notes.
    You can now apply your specified Quantize parameters to other MIDI clips without
    negotiating the dialogue box every time by pressing Cmd/Ctrl+U.

# THE GROOVE POOL

Using the Groove Pool, you can impose the timing and dynamics of one MIDI or audio clip
on another. Live includes a sizeable library of grooves (timing and volume 'maps'), but you can
capture the groove of any clip by right-clicking it and selecting Extract Groove(s). Doing this,
or double-clicking a library groove, loads it into the Groove Pool, which is opened and closed
using the 'wavy lines' button below the browser. Simply drag a groove from the Groove Pool

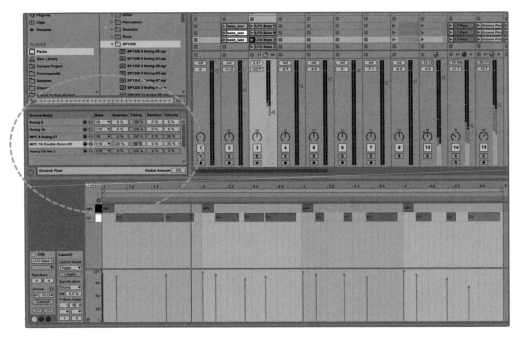

**Above**: Give one MIDI or audio clip the feel and timing of another with the Groove Pool.

on to any MIDI or warped audio clip to apply it. Various aspects of the groove are adjustable, including the strength with which its Timing and Velocity are mapped onto the target clip. Grooves are applied in real-time, but when you want to fully render a clip with the groove applied, hit the Commit button in the clip's Clip box.

## THE NOTES BOX

The Notes box houses a range of useful controls for adjusting the contents of the selected MIDI clip. If you can't see it in the Clip View, click the small 'musical notes' button at the bottom left.

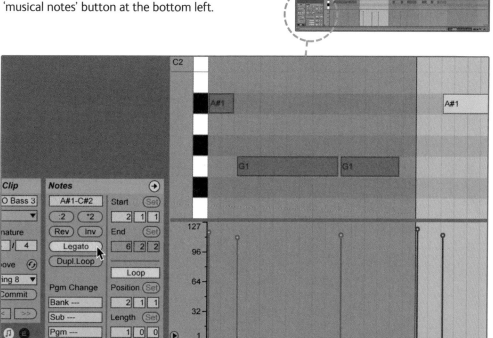

**Above:** Access a number of frequently used MIDI clip editing controls in the Notes box.

On the right of the Notes box are the same clip and loop Start and End controls as found in an audio clip's Sample box. The Duplicate Loop button doubles the length of the looped region within the clip and copies its contents. The rest of the controls affect selected notes, or all notes if none are selected, and comprise transposition, halving and doubling tempo, and stretching notes to lead contiguously into each other (Legato).

Hot Tip

**Type note names directly into the transposition field to change them.**

## MIDI Clip Envelopes and MIDI CCs

MIDI clips can be automated with Clip Envelopes, just like audio clips (*see* page 43).
The target categories listed in the Envelopes box's Device Chooser are slightly different,
though, in that MIDI clips lose the Clip option and gain the MIDI Ctrl entry.

With MIDI Ctrl selected, the Control Chooser offers 120 MIDI Continuous Controllers
(CCs). These are of primary relevance to hardware synths, which use them for real-time
parameter changes, but Pitch Bend, Modulation and certain others are also used with virtual
instruments. Some CCs are standardized – for instance, CC1 should always be assigned to
Modulation, and CC64 to Sustain – but most are freely assignable by the manufacturer.
What you can automate using MIDI CCs will depend entirely on the particulars of your
sound source.

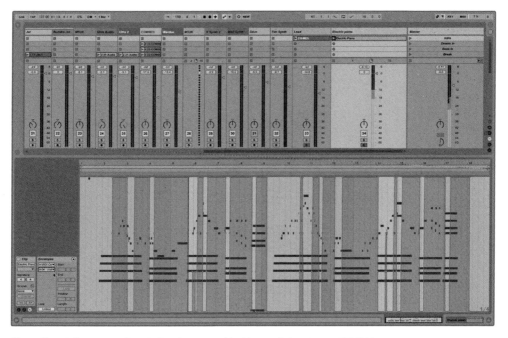

**Above:** The on/off movement of your keyboard's sustain pedal will be recorded into Live as MIDI CC64.

INSTRUMENTS & EFFECTS

# DEVICE BASICS

**Using built-in and third-party synths, samplers and effects, Live becomes a complete virtual music production and mixing environment in which all manner of amazing sounds can be created, manipulated, processed and brought together.**

## WHAT ARE DEVICES?

A device is a software module within Ableton Live that either generates or processes an audio signal, or non-destructively alters a stream of MIDI data, in real time.

### The Device Chain

Live includes an impressive array of built-in instruments, audio effects and MIDI effects, the exact number of which will depend on which version of the software you've invested in. On a

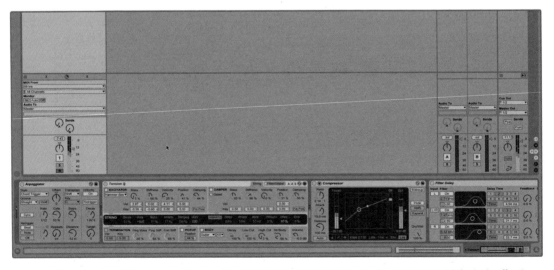

**Above:** Here's a MIDI track device chain: Arpeggiator (MIDI effect), Tension (instrument), Compressor and Filter Delay (audio effects).

MIDI track, the device chain created by dragging devices in from the browser comprises MIDI effects on the left, an instrument in the middle and audio effects on the right. An audio track's chain can only host audio effects.

### Hot Tip

**Multiple device chains can be combined in Racks – *see* page 63.**

## Instruments

Live's (up to) nine included virtual synthesizers and sample playback devices (plus the External Instrument device, for integrating hardware instruments) are in the Instrument category of the browser. Instruments are loaded on to MIDI tracks, where they receive MIDI (perhaps processed by one or more MIDI effects) and output audio to the mixer via any audio effects in the device chain.

## Audio Effects

The Audio Effects section of the device library contains up to 35 signal-processing modules, from compressors and EQs to reverbs, delays, modulation effects and much more. Audio effects work with both MIDI and audio tracks, transforming the output of the loaded instrument on the former and the currently playing audio clip on the latter.

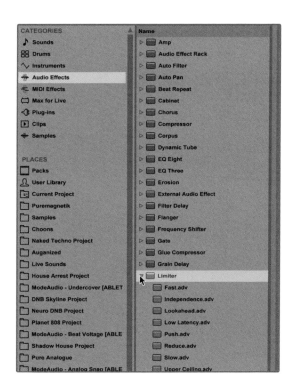

**Right:** Each device type has its own category in the Live browser.

# MIDI EFFECTS

Live's seven MIDI effects let you alter the MIDI note and Continuous Controller (CC) data used to trigger and automate software and hardware instruments. The devices include an arpeggiator, a randomizer, a scale 'snapper' and a chord generator, and are used to process MIDI clips and live input from a MIDI keyboard or other controller.

## Max for Live

Bundled with Live 9 Suite, Max for Live is a powerful device construction toolkit that includes an extensive collection of hugely creative prefab instruments and effects. Load them in from the Max for Live browser category.

**Below:** For weird and wonderful instruments, effects and MIDI processing, the Max for Live folder is the place to be.

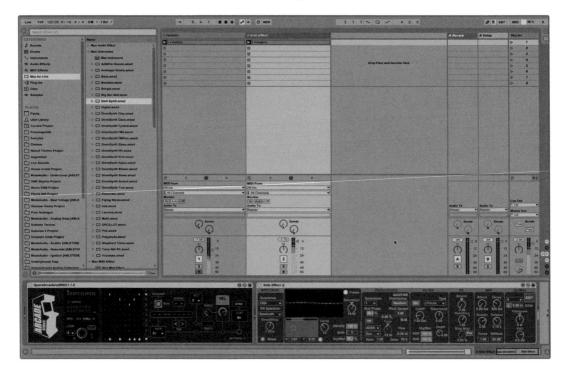

## Plugins

As well as its own instruments and audio effects, Ableton Live is compatible with third-party VST plugins on PC and VST and Audio Units plugins on Mac. There are literally thousands of them out there to be bought or downloaded for free, from classic synth emulations, drum machines and immense multisampled instruments to a panoply of amazing effects processors. Plugins are used just like Live's devices, but their interfaces open in dedicated windows rather than the Device View.

# DEVICE PRESETS

A preset is a snapshot of a device's parameter settings, stored as a file.

## Loading and Saving Presets

Clicking the arrow button next to any Live device in the browser reveals its presets. Double-click one to insert the device set to that preset into the currently selected track's device chain.

To save your own presets, make your tweaks to the parameters of the device in question, then click the Save Preset button on the device in the Device View – it looks like a floppy disk. The browser switches to the User Library folder, where a folder will have been created

with the device's name,
containing your preset,
the title of which is
selected for renaming.
Hit Enter to store the
preset in your User Library.

## Hot Tip

**Save a preset into any folder in the Places section
of the browser by dragging the device into it.**

## Hot-Swap Mode

Clicking the 'circular arrows' button on a device (or a sample slot in any sample-based instrument)
puts it into Hot-Swap mode. An orange text field appears at the top of the browser and the
preset folder for the device opens, where you can step through presets or samples using the
cursor and Enter keys. When you find a preset you like, hit Esc to exit Hot-Swap mode.

**Below:** Audition and load presets within a device in Hot-Swap mode.

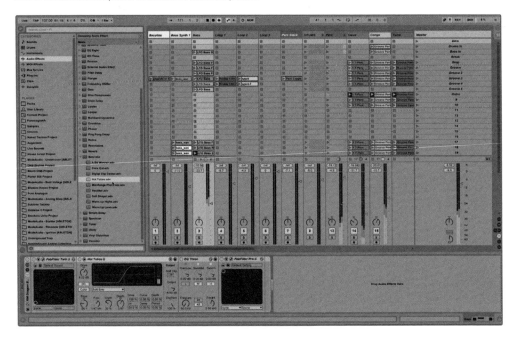

# RACKS

**Live's Racks enable the grouping of multiple devices in single presets, and the construction of complex parallel processing chains and layered instruments, complete with Macro controls for collective editing.**

## WHAT ARE RACKS?

There are three kinds of Rack – here's the lowdown.

### Drum Rack

A Drum Rack hosts a collection of up to 128 separate device chains, each one housed in its own 'pad' and triggered by a specific MIDI note, making it ideal for building drum kits.

**Hot Tip**

Up to 16 choke groups can be defined within a Drum Rack – use these to make closed hi-hats cut off open hi-hats for realism.

**Below:** Piece together drum kits of incredible complexity in the Drum Rack.

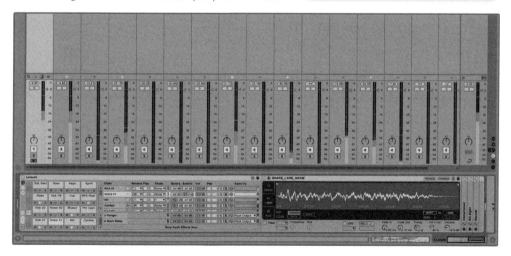

Every chain includes an instrument (dragging a sample in loads it into a 'Simpler') and effects (MIDI and audio), and/or further Racks of all kinds. The Drum Rack itself features six internal send effects busses, and each chain outputs to a dedicated mixer channel – click the triangular button at the top of the track to unfold them.

## Instrument Rack

An Instrument Rack contains a limitless number of device chains, each one comprising MIDI effects, an instrument and audio effects, and/or further nested Racks, and routed to its own channel in the mixer.

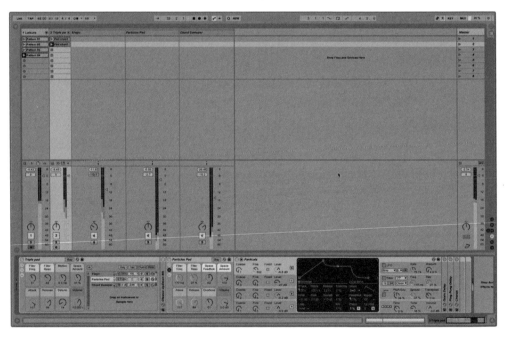

**Above:** This Instrument Rack contains three chains, each one loaded with its own Instrument Rack!

You can trigger all of the chains in an Instrument Rack together for layered sounds, or set each chain to discrete note and velocity ranges for keyboard splits – *see* pages

66–67. MIDI and audio processing is applied to all chains collectively by inserting MIDI and Audio Effects before and after the Rack, individually or in yet more Racks. There's really no limit to how intricate the architecture of an Instrument Rack can get, so go for it and let your imagination run wild!

## Audio and MIDI Effect Racks

The two simplest Rack types, Audio and MIDI Effect Racks, only contain effect devices and plugins, as well as further Racks of their own type for parallel processing. MIDI Effect Racks only work on MIDI tracks, obviously, while Audio Effect Racks can be placed on audio tracks and after instruments on MIDI tracks.

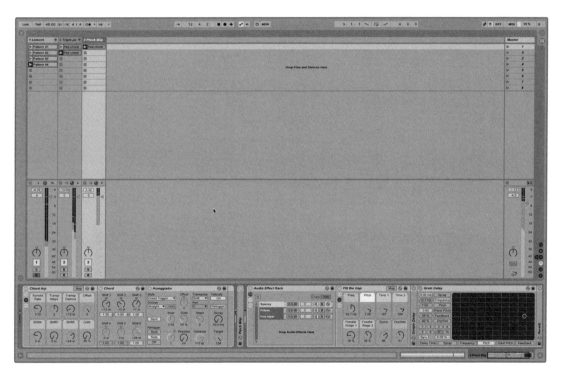

**Above:** Here, a MIDI Effect Rack processes the note input into an instrument (Plock Blip, collapsed), which outputs to an Audio Effect Rack.

# WORKING WITH RACKS

Racks make building and storing your own device chains easy.

## Parallel Chains

One of the chief benefits of Racks is that they allow you to layer multiple instruments and/or effects within a single device. In a regular device chain, an audio clip or single virtual instrument is processed by a series of effects, the output of one flowing to the input of the next. By stacking up chains in Instrument and Audio Effect Racks, though, any number of instruments can be triggered and processed together, and an audio signal can be processed by as many parallel effects chains as you like, with everything mixed down to a single stream at the end.

## The Chain List

The Chain List (invoked by clicking the middle of the three vertical buttons on the left-hand side of a Rack) is where the chains within a Rack are muted, soloed and have their volume, panning and – in Drum Racks – effects sends tweaked. Select a chain to make its contents

> ## Hot Tip
> You can drag chains and devices from Racks to other Racks and tracks – hold down the Option key while dragging to copy rather than move.

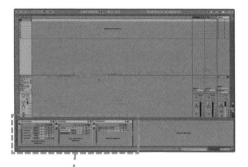

**Above:** Don't let the simple appearance of this folded-down nested Rack fool you – there's all manner of parallel processing and layering going on inside!

visible on the right, and activate the Auto Select button to have chains automatically selected as they receive input.

## Zones

Clicking the Key, Vel or Chain button in an Instrument, MIDI Effect or Audio Effect (Chain only) Rack opens the Key Zone Editor, Velocity Zone Editor or Chain Select Editor. The Key and Velocity Zone Editors let you set the input note and velocity range for each chain in an Instrument Rack, outside which the chain won't trigger. To set a range, drag the ends of the red or green bar, and to fade the chain in and/or out (increasing and decreasing the input note velocity), drag the ends of the thin bar above.

The Chain Select Editor lets you switch between chains by dragging the (MIDI- and Macro-assignable) orange Chain Selector handle at the top.

**Below:** Here, we have an Instrument Rack's Key Zone Editor on the left, and an Audio Effect Rack's Chain Select Editor on the right. The Chain Selector is assigned to a Macro, as indicated by a green dot.

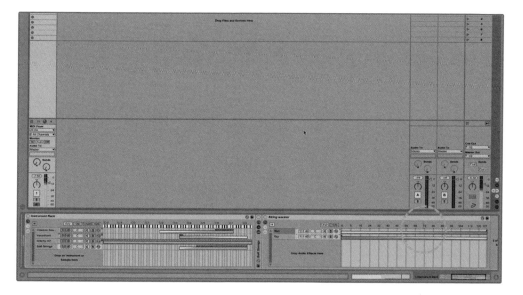

## Macro Controls

At the left-hand end of every Rack are eight assignable Macro knobs. If you can't see them, click the topmost of the three vertical buttons. Each Macro can be linked to any number of controls from all of the devices in the Rack, giving ready access to groups of instrument and effect parameters in a single location. For hands-on tweaking, assign Macros to your MIDI control surface (*see* page 103).

To tie a device control to a Macro, first click the Map button at the top of the Macro panel, then the parameter you want to assign, then the Map button under the Macro. Press Map again to exit mapping mode. Macro assignments are indicated by green dots on assigned parameters, and the Min/Max ranges of all Macro assignments are adjustable in the Macro Mappings panel that replaces the browser when in Map mode.

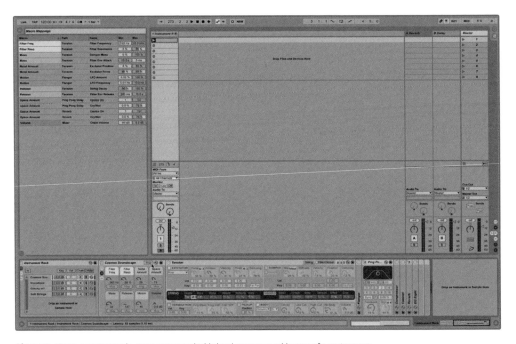

**Above:** In Macro mapping mode, every parameter highlighted green is a viable target for assignment.

# HOW TO MAKE AN INSTRUMENT RACK

1. Let's walk through the process of making and storing a simple Instrument Rack. To start, we drag the Instrument Rack device on to a MIDI track from the Instruments category of the browser.

2. We want to layer two synths as a single sound, so we start by dragging an Analog preset into the Instrument Rack, then open the Chain List and drag an Operator preset in. Now we have two chains. Dragging effects devices into each chain processes the two synths independently, while a Filter Delay placed after the Rack processes both together. An Arpeggiator MIDI Effect in front of the Rack arpeggiates the incoming MIDI notes for both.

3. Selecting everything in the Device View – Arpeggiator, Instrument Rack and subsequent effects – and pressing Cmd/Ctrl+G groups the whole lot into a top-level Instrument Rack, which we can save into the User library by clicking its Save Preset button.

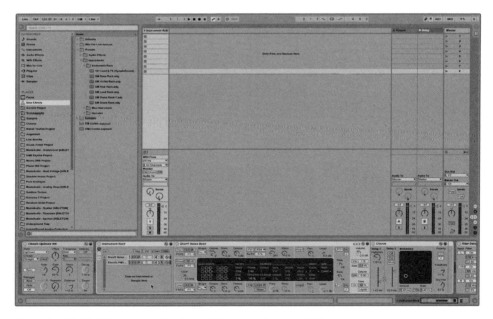

**Above:** Press Cmd/Ctrl+G to group together all selected devices in an Instrument Rack.

# DEVICE HIGHLIGHTS

**Ableton Live comes with a plethora of superb instruments and effects, although how many of them you get depends on which version of the software you've plumped for. Here are our favourites.**

## FIVE OF LIVE'S BEST INSTRUMENTS

Here are our top five, they're not all exclusive to the top-of-the-range version of Live!

### Sampler (Suite)

A powerhouse of sample playback and processing, Sampler can load prefab multisample libraries in just about any format, and makes building your own a breeze. Separate Sustain and Release Loops, a morphing multimode filter and extensive modulation capabilities give it the sound design chops, and the pop-up Zone editor is the icing on the cake.

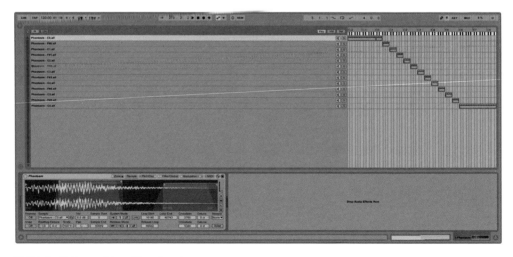

**Above:** Sampler is powerful, versatile and easy to use.

## Drum Rack (Intro, Standard, Suite)

With its peerless ability to bring together sampled and synthesized sources, Drum Rack gives you everything you need to create drum kits of limitless scope and scale. To open the gates to beat-making heaven, team it up with Ableton's Push 2 MIDI controller.

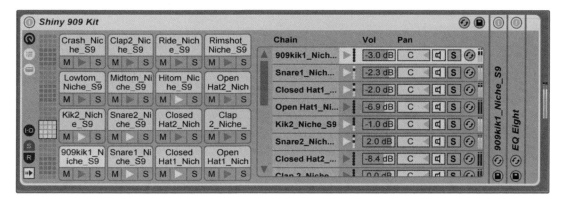

**Above**: Build your own drum kits in Drum Rack.

## Simpler (Intro, Standard, Suite)

Live's bread-and-butter sampler, Simpler loads prefab multisamples for playback, and enables deep editing and manipulation of your own one-shots and loops. It's also the default module used to host samples in Drum Rack pads.

**Above**: When Sampler is more than you need, Simpler gets the job done.

## Analog and Operator (Suite)

Live's analogue and FM (frequency modulation) synths might seem basic compared to much of the third-party plugin competition, but they give Live Suite owners plenty of options when it comes to generating electronic tones, and both sound great.

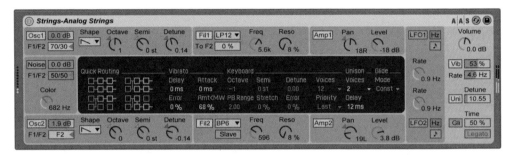

**Above:** Analog is a simple but effective virtual analogue synthesizer.

**Above:** Operator makes the potentially head-swimming concept of FM synthesis approachable.

# Hot Tip

**Right-click a clip and select Freeze Track to render it as audio, disabling all effects and instruments on the track and reducing Live's CPU load. Right-click again and click Unfreeze Track to reverse the process, or Flatten to permanently turn it into an audio clip.**

# FOUR OF LIVE'S BEST AUDIO EFFECTS

Audio effects used well can put an entirely new spin on a composition. Here are the four we like playing with the most.

## Glue Compressor (Standard, Suite)

This special Live-exclusive edition of Cytomic's acclaimed The Glue emulates the bus compressor from an Eighties SSL mixing console. Intended for use on Group Tracks and the Master Track, Glue Compressor is particularly adept at bringing cohesion (that's the glue!) to drum kits and full mixes. Like several of Live's effects, it also features a sidechain input, for compressing one sound based on the dynamic profile of another.

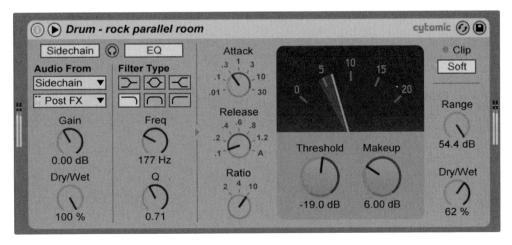

**Above:** Get those drum busses sounding tight and punchy with Glue Compressor.

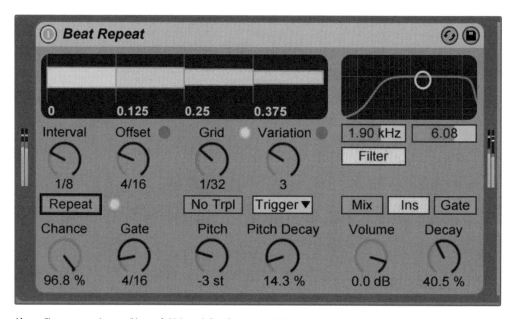

**Above:** Electronica producers will have a field day with Beat Repeat's mad glitching.

## Beat Repeat
### (Intro, Standard, Suite)

A favourite of electronica producers, Beat Repeat periodically captures slices of the input signal in a buffer and replays them for controlled or randomized glitch effects, stutters, micro-loops, etc. Slices and repeats can be pitched, filtered and decayed, and three mix modes determine how the original signal and repeats are combined.

## Saturator
### (Intro, Standard, Suite)

A touch of distortion adds edge and grit to any sound, and Live's Saturator is a master of the art, tooled up for everything from subtle fuzz and warming to all-out sonic decimation. Six fixed shapes cover the analogue-style and digital basics, while the editable Waveshaper lets you design your own curves.

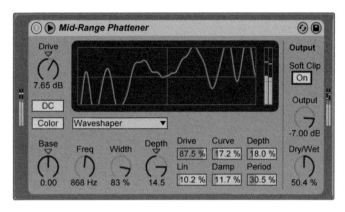

**Above:** Heat those signals up with the amazing Saturator distortion device.

## EQ Eight (Standard, Suite)

Each of EQ Eight's eight parametric bands can operate as any one of eight filter types – low/high Shelf, bell, 12dB/48dB low/high-pass, or notch – with optional Adaptive Q emulating the proportional resonance you might get with an analogue EQ. Edit the curve directly in the display/frequency analyser, which can be popped out to fill the Session/Arrangement View area, filling the device interface with old-school control knobs.

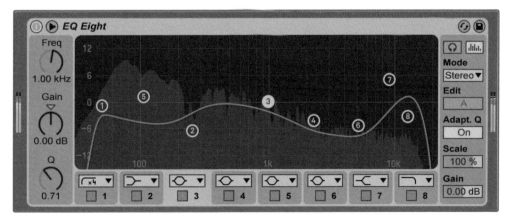

**Above:** A quality EQ is a must at every stage of the production process – EQ Eight more than qualifies.

# FOUR OF LIVE'S BEST MIDI EFFECTS

Last but not least, these fab four can turn a few instruments into a polyphonic orchestra!

**Above:** Turn chords into sequential melody lines with Arpeggiator.

## Arpeggiator (Intro, Standard, Suite)

Arpeggiator separates an incoming MIDI chord into its component notes and plays them back as an arpeggio – that is, a series of rhythmically spaced-apart single notes. A wide range of playback styles is included, and control is given over the playback speed, note duration and swing of the arpeggio, as well as transposition and velocity fading.

## Chord (Intro, Standard, Suite)

Every note entering this MIDI effect is stacked with up to six more notes and output as a chord. The pitch offset of each added note from the triggering one is set anywhere from -36 to +36 semitones (three octaves up or down), and their velocities can be scaled from 1–200%.

**Right:** Turn melody lines into chord sequences with Chord!

**Right:** Bring the element of chance into play with the Random MIDI effect.

## Random (Intro, Standard, Suite)

Work a bit of chaos into your compositions with the Random MIDI effect. The Chance dial determines the likelihood of the pitch of an incoming note being randomized, while Choices and Scale set the number and range of possible random values that might result. Randomization can be upwards, downwards or both, and switching to Alt mode steps through the possible values in fixed order instead. Crazy!

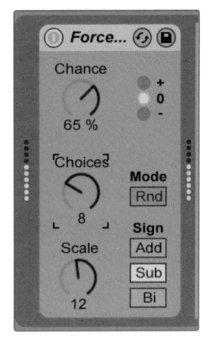

**Below:** Compress and gate MIDI clips with Velocity.

## Velocity (Intro, Standard, Suite)

An ingenious dynamics processor for MIDI notes, Velocity offers an array of controls for remapping input velocity (on the X axis of the display) to output velocity (Y). Shape the dynamic response curve and set a random range of variance around it, filter notes out if they don't fall within a stated range, constrain output to a single velocity regardless of input, and more.

ARRANGING A TRACK

# THE ARRANGEMENT VIEW

While the Session View enables freeform jamming with audio and MIDI loops and clips, the Arrangement View is a linear song-construction environment of the kind found in most other DAWs.

## FIRST STEPS

Turn the musical sketches made in the Session View into a finished song.

### Operational Basics

**To switch between the Session and Arrangement Views**, hit the Tab key on your keyboard. In the Arrangement View, the playhead progresses through your Live Set on a timeline from left to right, playing it back just like a multitrack tape deck, with the tracks stacked up horizontally, rather than arranged vertically as in the Session View.

**Unfold tracks** by clicking the arrow buttons next to their names, and widen them further by dragging their bottom boundaries. The right-hand end

of each track contains the mixer controls and automation menus, and the Arrangement Overview at the top shows the entire arrangement in miniature.

**To zoom in and out**, press the +/- keys, or drag up and down in the Arrangement Overview or the grey area immediately below. Double-click the Arrangement Overview to zoom all the way out. To scroll the arrangement around, drag in the same areas or use your mousewheel or trackpad.

Below the timeline, the **Scrub Area** houses the Arrangement loop brace, which functions just like its counterpart in the Clip View, cycling playback when the Loop switch in the Control Bar is activated. The loop brace also sets punch-in and -out points for recording. Clicking in the Scrub Area starts playback from that point, and if the Set is already playing, the jump to the new playback position will be quantized for seamless continuity.

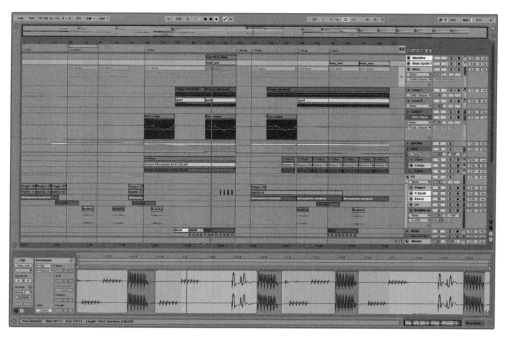

**Above:** Live's Arrangement View is where you build your finished tracks.

Finally, if you enter the Arrangement
View while clips are playing in the
Session View, the tracks containing
those clips will be greyed out, as a
track can only play from one View at a
time. Clicking the triangle button at the
right-hand end of an 'overridden' track
reactivates it and stops playback of the
Session View clip. Clicking the Back to
Arrangement button at the right-hand
end of the Scrub Area reactivates the
whole Arrangement.

## Hot Tip

Right-click the Scrub Area and
select Add Locator to insert a
nameable section marker. Call it
'Verse', 'Chorus' or whatever you
like. Double-click a Locator to start
playback from that point, and
right-click to access various options.

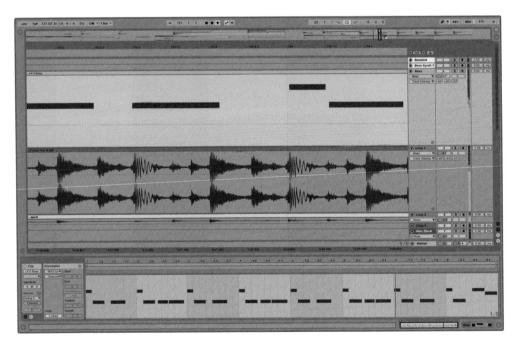

**Above:** Zoom in and out by dragging in the Arrangement Overview.

## Transferring Clips to the Arrangement View

One way to start an arrangement is to jam around in the Session View and capture the results in the Arrangement View. Click the Arrangement Record button in the Session View's Control Bar and start triggering clips and scenes, automating devices and plugins, etc., roughly as you want your finished track to be. Flip to the Arrangement View and you'll see that everything has been recorded exactly as it happened!

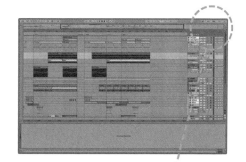

Alternatively, select some clips in the Session View and hold the mouse button down, press Tab to switch to the Arrangement View, then drag them into place (or drag them directly on to the

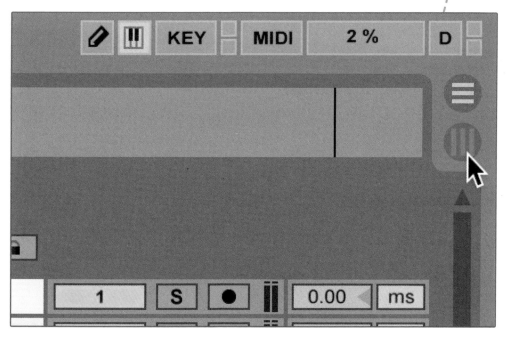

**Above:** Drag clips to the Arrangement or Session View Selectors to transfer them between the two.

Arrangement View Selector button, top right). Dragging clips works in the opposite direction – Arrangement to Session View – too.

### Recording in the Arrangement View

As well as recording Session View performances and dragging clips in, you can also record directly into the Arrangement View.

With your audio interface and/or MIDI controller(s) set up in Live's Preferences and any number of MIDI and/or audio tracks armed for recording, click the Arrangement Record button to start playback of the Set (with a count-in) and record the signals received by every armed track. Click Record again or hit the space bar to stop. Clicking Record when the Set is already playing back starts recording at the playback position.

To 'punch in' and 'out' – that is, automatically start and/or stop recording at specific points on the timeline (to replace a few bum notes in the middle of an otherwise solid performance, for example) – set the loop brace markers to encompass the timespan you want to record into, then activate the Punch-In and/or Punch-Out switches in the Control Bar. With both active, recording starts when the playhead reaches the Loop Start marker and stops when it reaches the Loop End marker.

To overdub new MIDI notes into an existing clip, as opposed to overwriting the whole thing, activate the MIDI Arrangement Overdub Button, to the right of the Arrangement Record button.

Recording multiple passes in the Loop range results in a single recording – position the Start/End markers in the Clip View to select a portion for playback.

**Below:** Here, we're recording to an audio track and a MIDI track at the same time. We've punched in, too, to ensure the recordings start at exactly the point we want.

## Hot Tip

**Instantly turn a section of your arrangement into a Session View Scene by selecting it and choosing Consolidate Time to New Scene from the Create menu.**

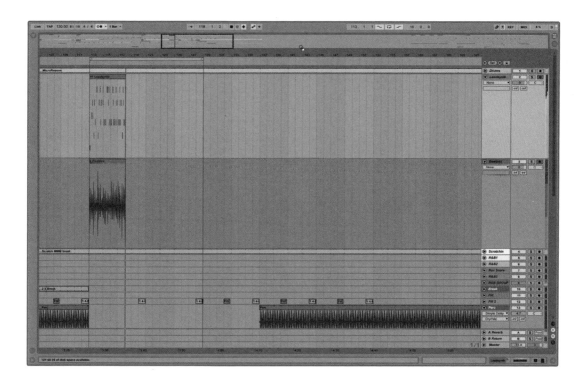

# ARRANGING AND EDITING CLIPS

**Arranging tracks effectively and 'correctly' is an art in itself, but Live gives you all the tools you need.**

## LAYING OUT A TRACK

We don't have anywhere near the space for a comprehensive guide to musical arrangement, but here are some pointers:

- **Establish a structure**: There are several tried and tested structures that you should probably stick to when arranging tracks, so rather than try to figure them out on your own, Google 'song arrangement tips/template/tutorials/etc.' and educate yourself. Whether to have one verse or two before the chorus, how to place a middle eight, how to construct an effective drop and so on – these are all things you need to know.

- **Don't over-complicate**: Keep the amount of instrumentation playing at any given time as minimal as possible without compromising the intent of the track in order to make mixing easier and avoid frequency clutter.

- **Trust your instincts!** If a part just doesn't sound right and ten minutes of editing and processing hasn't begun to fix it, ditch it and either record it again or replace it with something else.

- **Consider the DJ**: If your track is intended for use within a DJ set, be sure to place at least 16 bars of drums (not necessarily on their own) at the start and end for the DJ to beat match with when mixing it in and out.

- **Borrow ideas**: Don't have any qualms about using the arrangement of a commercial track that you love as a template for your own project.

○ **Give it an ending**: Only fade your track out at the end if you really can't think of any other way to wrap it up.

**Above**: Make life easy for the DJ by giving your track a percussive intro and outro.

## SELECTING CLIPS AND TIME RANGES

To select a clip for moving and editing with the various functions in the right-click and menu bar menus, simply click it. To select a region of time within a clip, unfold the track by clicking the triangular button next to its name and drag your selection within the waveform or MIDI overview. Now you can click or drag the title bar of the selected region to move, copy or cut it as if it were a separate clip.

To select multiple clips and/or sections of clips, or a period of time on the timeline for cutting/copying/pasting, duplication or deletion (via the Edit menu), drag a selection box. To select everything within the loop brace, press Cmd/Ctrl+Shift+L, and to loop the current selection, press Cmd/Ctrl+L.

The dragged selection range snaps to the grid (*see* next page), as well as the starts and ends of clips.

## Hot Tip

To unfold all of the tracks in your Set at once, hold the Option key while clicking the unfold button (a black triangle in a circle) of any one of them.

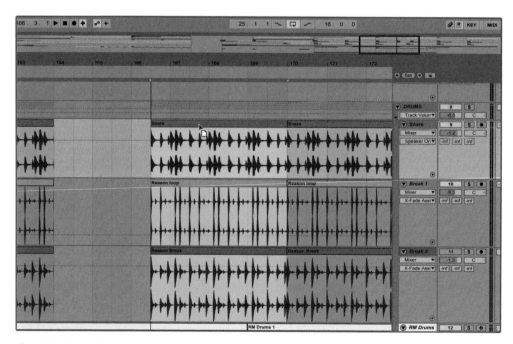

**Above:** Box-drag to select regions within multiple clips at once for moving or copying.

# THE EDITING GRID

Snap to Grid and its associated functions are located in the Arrangement View Options menu, but each also has a keyboard shortcut. With Snap to Grid turned on (Cmd/Ctrl+4), clips 'magnetically' snap to the visible grid lines when moved, the resolution of which is displayed at the bottom right of the Arrangement View. The grid resolution can be set absolutely or linked to the zoom level – the further out you zoom, the wider the spacing of the grid lines. Toggle between the two behaviours with Cmd/Ctrl+5.

Whichever mode you're in, Cmd/Ctrl+1 and Cmd/Ctrl+2 double and halve the grid resolution respectively, and Cmd/Ctrl+3 switches between triplet and regular grids. Hold the Cmd/Ctrl key to temporarily turn snap off when moving or resizing clips. All of the above applies to the Clip View editing grid too.

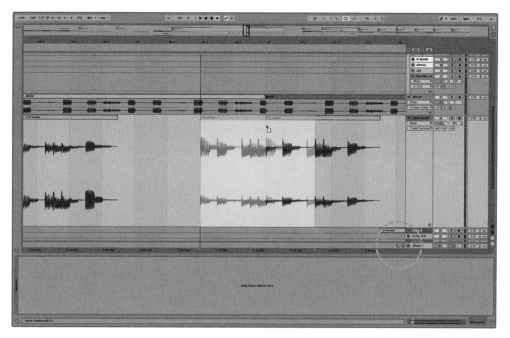

**Above:** With the grid resolution set to 1/4, clips always land on the beat when moved or copied.

## Resizing, Splitting and Repeating Clips

1. To resize a clip, drag its left- or right-hand edge. The clip acts like a 'window' on the audio or MIDI data it contains, which stays where it is unless the clip as a whole is moved.

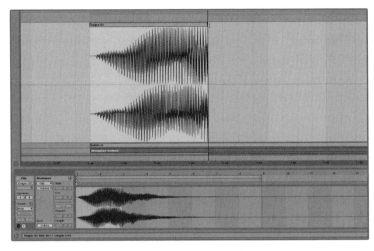

**Above**: Step 1: Dragging the right-hand edge of a clip shortens the playback region.

2. To split a clip in two, unfold its track, then click at the point you want the split to occur and press Cmd/Ctrl+E to invoke the Edit > Split menu option. To split a clip in three, select a region within it, then invoke Split, or just drag the selected region away from the other two.

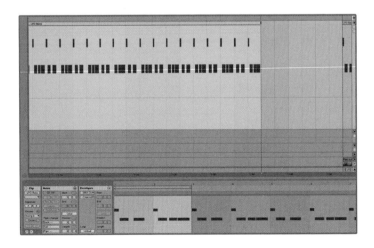

3. To repeatedly loop a clip along the timeline, rather than copy and paste it over and over again, activate Loop in the Clip View Sample or Notes box and drag either edge.

**Left**: Step 3: Activate Loop in the Notes box and drag the edge of a clip to repeat it.

## Clip Fades

1. Every audio clip in the Arrangement View is automatically faded in and out at either end, and the lengths and shapes of these fades can be adjusted. To reveal the fade envelope for a clip, unfold the track and select Fades from its track's Device Chooser, just below the track name, or right-click the clip itself and select Show Fades.

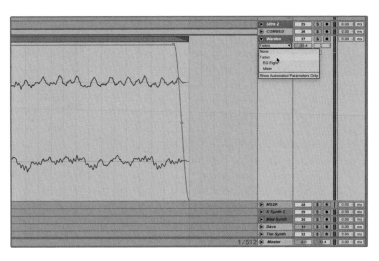

**Above**: Step 1: Select Fades in a track's Device Chooser to edit the automatic Arrangement View clip fades.

2. Drag the handle at the top of the fade curve to change its length, and the handle in the middle to adjust the shape of the curve.

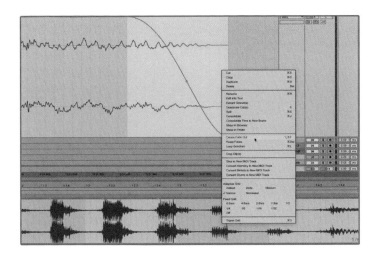

3. Alternatively, select a region within the audio clip, right-click it and select Create Fade In/ Out or press Cmd/ Ctrl+Option+F.

**Left**: Step 3: To create a fade directly on a clip, right-click it and select Fade In or Fade Out.

## Clip Crossfades

By default, overlapping one audio clip with another on the same track causes the two to play consecutively as they appear on the timeline. With Fades selected in the track's Device Chooser, however, dragging the fade handle of one clip into the other defines a crossfade between the two. Drag the crossover point to change the crossfade shape. Alternatively, select a region across the two clips and press Cmd/Ctrl+Alt+F.

**Above:** Ableton's virtual crossfader mimics the effect of traditional crossfader switches on a mixing desk.

**Above:** Drag the crossfade crossover point to shape the curves.

## Consolidating Clips

Selecting a region in the Arrangement View and hitting the Consolidate command in the right-click or Edit menu (Cmd/Ctrl+J) renders everything in the selection into a single clip per track of that track's type. For example, in the screenshot below, the big clip was originally a series of smaller clips, like those on the tracks above and below. Consolidating them rendered that section of the track as a new audio file.

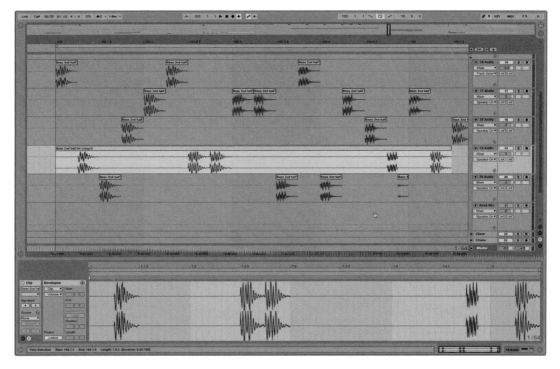

**Above:** Here, the multiple audio clips on the highlighted region have been consolidated into a single clip.

Consolidating MIDI clips glues them together and/or splits them apart, depending on the coverage of the selected region. In a nutshell, all MIDI data within the selection is fused into a single clip, and all data outside is sliced off at the boundaries of the selection.

THE MIXDOWN

# MIXING A TRACK IN LIVE

**Mixing is the stage of the production process when your musical arrangement is sonically sculpted and shaped into a finished track, through the adjustment of parameters and the application of effects.**

## THE MIXER

Live's mixer is integrated directly into both the Session and Arrangement Views – if you can't see it, press Cmd/Ctrl+Option+M. The Arrangement View positions numeric mixer controls for each (unfolded) track in a small area at the right-hand end, thus prioritizing space for the arrangement area. The Session View, on the other hand, presents a more traditional mixer, with

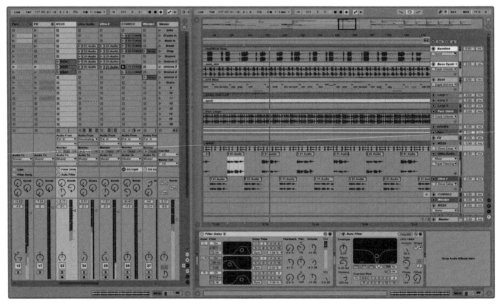

**Above:** With two Live windows open at once, you can mix and arrange at the same time!

vertical faders, knobs for pans and sends, etc., and is thus the preferred View for mixing once the arrangement is done. To extend the channel faders and meters, drag their top boundary lines upwards.

## Levels, Panning, Mute and Solo

Adjusting the vertical slider at the bottom of a track in the Session View, or the right-most number field in the Arrangement View, raises and lowers the volume of that track, as visualized in the green meters alongside – see page 102. The Pan control positions the output of the track in the stereo field – that is, between the left and right channels. To mute a track, click the yellow Track Activator button at the bottom, turning it grey; to hear a track in isolation, click the Solo button below the Track Activator. A good way to start a mix is to set all levels to zero and pan controls to the centre, then introduce and position each part one at a time – drums, then bass, then guitars, and so on.

**Hot Tip**

Select Second Window from the View menu to open an additional Live window for positioning on the same or a secondary monitor. The extra window is particularly useful for running the Session View mixer alongside the Arrangement View.

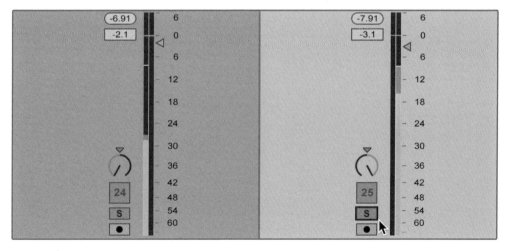

**Above:** These two tracks have been hard-panned left and right, and are currently soloed.

# EFFECTS AND GROUPS

Polish and enhance your sounds, and gather related parts together for processing and mixing convenience.

## Insert Effects

Insert effects are signal processing devices and plugins 'inserted' directly into tracks in order to change their sounds to a lesser or greater extent. To insert an effect, drag it directly on to a track from the browser. It will appear in the track's device chain, as well as the Session View device slots, which are revealed by clicking the Show/Hide Device Slots button.

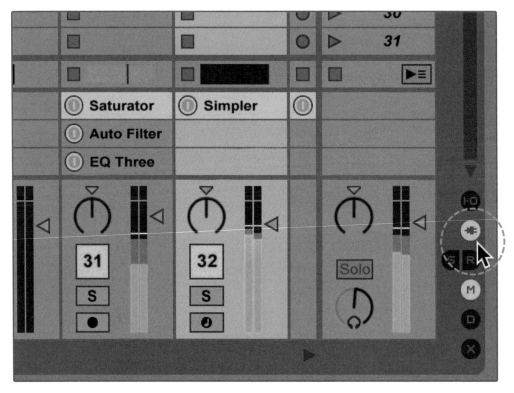

**Above:** Here, you can see the Device Slots for two tracks and the Show/Hide button on the right.

## Compression and EQ

Of all the effects that are called on during the mixing stage, compression and equalization are probably the most important. While chorus, flanging and tremolo might be used to make elements of a track sound interesting and exciting, compressors and EQs are primarily called on to sit them comfortably in the mix in terms of frequency content and dynamic range. Using them effectively and 'correctly' requires education and practice, so if you want your mixes to sound as good as they possibly can, make the time and effort to investigate these essential tools. Handily, Live is blessed with some excellent compressor and EQ devices – *see* pages 73–75 for details of the best ones.

**Above:** Live's Compressor and EQ Eight devices are your best mixing friends.

## Return Tracks and Send Controls

While insert effects process their host tracks directly, Return Tracks (revealed/hidden with Cmd/Ctrl+Option+R) are used to process multiple sounds with the same shared effects (main and backing vocals through a single reverb, for example). A Live Set can contain up to 12 Return Tracks (Create > Insert Return Track to add one), each with its own effects chain. To tap a track's output off to a Return Track, raise the corresponding Send dial/field above/below the level fader/field (revealed/hidden with Cmd/Ctrl+Option+S), depending on which View you're in. The signal from that track will appear in the Return Track mixer channel at a level determined by the Send control, as well as its own channel. Repeat for as many tracks as you want to send to that Return Track.

The Pre/Post buttons on the Master Track (Session View) or Return Tracks (Arrangement View) switch between tapping the source signal pre-fader (the send amount is set only by the Send control) and post-

### Hot Tip

**Return Tracks can send to each other and even themselves. Their Send controls are disabled by default to prevent feedback – activate them by right-clicking and selecting Enable Send. Beware: routing a track to itself can damage your speakers and hearing!**

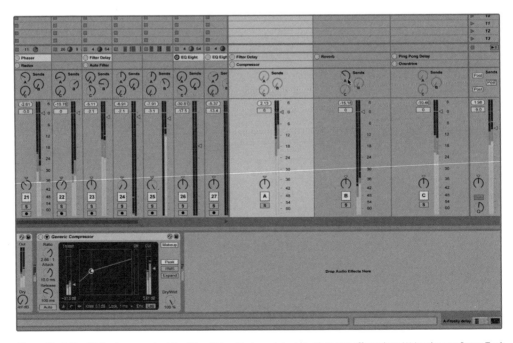

**Above:** The A, B and C Sends on every track feed three Return Tracks, each loaded with its own effects chain. We've also sent Return Track B gently back into Return Track A.

fader (changing the level of the track affects the send amount). The Mix controls for devices and plugins on Return Tracks should always be set to 100% wet, so as to avoid duplication of the dry signal from the source track.

## Group Tracks

A Group Track is analogous to a 'folder' containing multiple audio and MIDI tracks – the individual elements of a drum kit or string section, say, also known as a 'submix'. Grouping tracks gives you a single volume fader with which to level them collectively, and lets you apply effects to the whole lot by inserting them directly into the Group Track or using its Send controls. To fold multiple tracks down into a single Group Track, select them and press Cmd/Ctrl+G. Unfold the Group by clicking the triangular button next to its name, and add to and remove tracks from it by dragging them in and out. To collapse the Group, select it and press Cmd/Ctrl+Shift+G.

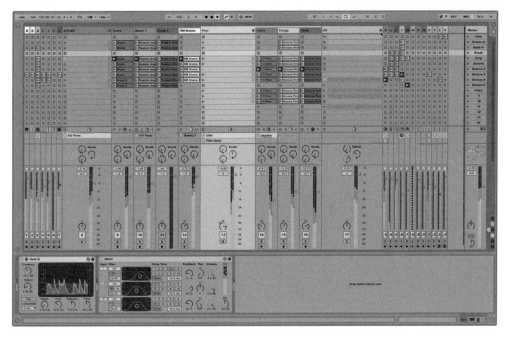

**Above:** Here, you can clearly see our unfolded Drums and Percussion Groups, and the folded-away FX Group.

# METERING AND THE MASTER TRACK

Wrapping up our tour of the mixer, we come to the last stage of the signal flow.

## The Master Track

Occupying the right-hand edge of the Session View and bottom edge of the Arrangement View, the Master Track is the final destination to which every audio signal in your Set is ultimately routed. Insert mastering effects – *see* page 106 – and use the level fader to control the overall volume of the mix (generally only to prevent clipping of the output).

## Metering

The level meters on every audio-outputting track show both peak (dark green) and RMS (Root Mean Square – bright green) levels, the first being the absolute level at any given moment, the second the average level over time, which more accurately represents perceived loudness. Drag the top boundary line of any meter to extend it upwards, revealing the Peak Level display, which shows the highest level that Track has reached since playback started. If this goes above 0 and turns yellow (and the meter itself crosses the zero line and enters the red), you should bring the level of the track down. If the Master Track itself goes into the red, nasty digital clipping will occur – to remedy this, bring down the levels of tracks within the mix or lower the Master fader.

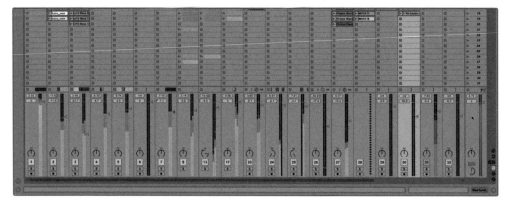

**Above:** If your Master Track meter looks like this, you need to lower the Master fader or, preferably, the other track and Group faders in the mix.

# AUTOMATION

**Build dynamic movement into your Set by recording or drawing automation. Here, we show you how.**

## RECORDING AUTOMATION WITH A MIDI CONTROLLER

The most fun and intuitive way to create a mixer or device automation envelope (curve) is to record it 'live' using the mouse or a MIDI controller. To assign the knobs, buttons and/ or faders on your controller to the parameters you want to automate, enter MIDI Map

**Above:** Here, the level faders of the four tracks within our Drums Group, and the Group fader, have been assigned to MIDI CCs 24–28.

mode by pressing Cmd/Ctrl+M or clicking the MIDI button in the Control Bar, click the target parameter to select it, then move the knob/fader on your hardware. The MIDI CC output by that knob/fader now controls the parameter, and hitting Record captures your real-time manipulations of it as an editable envelope. Play the track back to see your recorded automation envelope in action!

# EDITING AND DRAWING MIX AUTOMATION ENVELOPES

1. To edit a recorded automation envelope or draw a new one by hand in the Arrangement View, start by selecting the parameter you want to work with from the Device and Control Choosers under the track name. Parameters with automation envelopes already in place

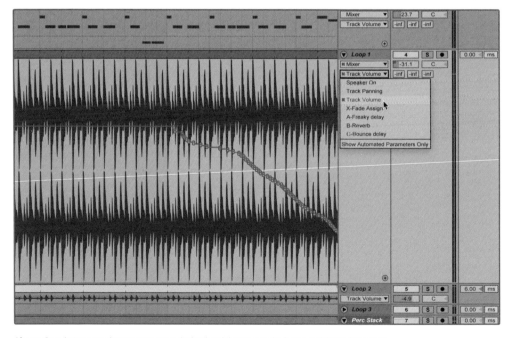

**Above:** Step 1: Automated parameters are marked with red dots in a track's Device and Control Choosers.

will have a red dot next to them. The envelope appears on the track as a red curve, or a dotted straight line if no automation has yet been applied.

2. Drag the envelope breakpoints around to reshape the envelope (select a region on the track to move multiple breakpoints). Alternatively, press the B key to switch to pencil mode, deactivate Snap to Grid (Cmd/Ctrl+4) and draw/edit your envelope freehand.

**Hot Tip**

**If your MIDI controller is listed in Live's MIDI Preferences Control Surface menu, it automatically maps to parameters in Live – see the Live User Manual for details.**

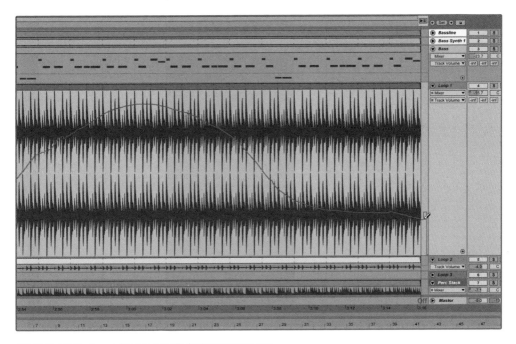

**Above:** Step 2: Use the pencil tool to manually draw automation curves.

# MASTERING AND EXPORTING

**Although using finalizing effects on the master bus isn't really something you should try unless you know what you're doing, a little bit of mix bus limiting can work wonders.**

## MASTER LIMITING

Attempting to run effects on the Master Track isn't something we'd advise unless you're schooled in the art of mastering. You're more likely to damage the sound than improve it, so leaving the Master Track device-free and sending your rendered song to a dedicated online mastering service such as Landr, eMastered or Abbey Road Online Mastering is a much better idea. However, it can be worth trying a touch of gentle limiting (using the best limiter plugin you can afford) to catch excessive peaks and increase loudness. Equally, if you feel a little low- or high-end boost is required, a bit of subtle shelving EQ could be effective.

## EXPORTING THE MIX

With the mix done, it's time to render it as a single stereo audio file for mastering or file compression and distribution. In the Arrangement View, set the loop brace to encompass the whole song, then press Cmd/Ctrl+Shift+R to open the Export Audio dialogue box. Select Master in the Rendered Track menu; choose your File Type (WAV or AIFF); set Sample Rate and Bit Depth to 44100 and 16-bit, or 96000 and 24- or 32-bit if your track is due to be mastered; turn Dither off for subsequent mastering; activate Upload to SoundCloud if required (a separate dialogue box will open for this after export); and hit Export. The mix is rendered to your location of choice and you're done! Finally, select File > Collect All and Save to bring all external audio files in the Set into the project folder for archiving.

**Below:** Turn Dither off in the Export Audio/Video dialogue box if your track is destined for the mastering studio.

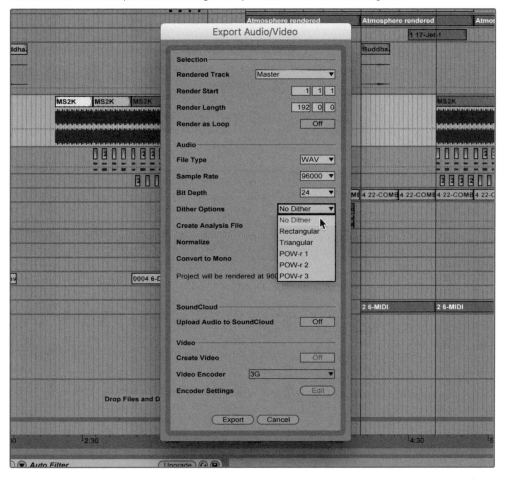

PLAYING LIVE

# DJING WITH LIVE

**With its ability to load full tracks as clips and keep everything in sync at all times, the Session View makes Live one of the most powerful digital DJing platforms around.**

## PREPARING YOUR LIVE SET

You can warp tracks on the fly while you play to get them in time, but it's far safer to get them all sorted before the gig.

### Auto-Warping Tracks

Live keeps all your tracks locked to the beat so that they all launch in time with each other and automatically timestretch to the project tempo, but in order for that to happen, they need to be properly warped in the first place. Drag a full track into a Session View clip slot and Live will do its best to warp it automatically, aligning its detected beats with the grid. How successful it is will depend on the source material: solid, four-to-the-floor tracks (house, techno, etc.) will generally warp perfectly, but less rhythmically concrete material might need tweaking. You can see and edit the Warp Markers in the Clip View.

If Live warps a track correctly but gets the position of the initial downbeat (the first beat) wrong, place the Start Marker precisely on the downbeat (zoom in for accuracy), right-click it and select Set 1.1.1 Here. If the Warp Markers are incorrectly placed throughout, you'll need to go through the whole track from left to right, double-clicking above the waveform to add Warp Markers on significant beats (the downbeat of every eight- or 16-bar section, for example) and moving them to the right points on the timeline. For really irregular tracks, you may have to warp every bar, or even individual beats within a bar, but once it's done, clicking Save in the Sample box stores the Warp Markers with the audio file for future reuse.

# Hot Tip

**For optimum results when warping full tracks, use Complex or Complex Pro Warp mode. To have tracks pitch up and down with tempo changes, like vinyl, run them in Re-Pitch mode.**

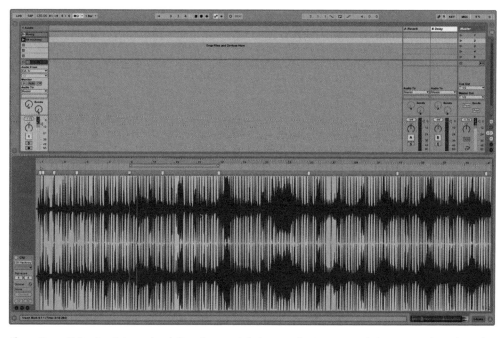

**Above:** Live couldn't quite nail the warping of this track automatically, but manually pinning every eight-bar section to the timeline with Warp Markers took no time at all.

# LAYING OUT TRACKS AND SCENES IN THE SESSION VIEW

With all the songs (we'd best start calling them that, to differentiate them from Live's tracks) in your DJ set warped, the next step is to lay them out in clip slots on tracks in the Session View in whatever way suits you best. If you intend to never do more than crossfading from the end of one song into the start of another – like a regular two-deck DJ – you could simply create two tracks in a Set and drag songs in from the browser on to either as required during the gig. If you're planning to mix more than two songs (perhaps setting up loops within multiple songs on the fly and building grooves with them, or just looping the beat from one song and a percussion break from another under the full length of a third), create as many audio tracks as you might need, and drag songs on to them in Scenes, roughly predicting the combinations you might use. This doesn't have to be in any sense 'final' – you can move clips around within the Set while you perform, of course.

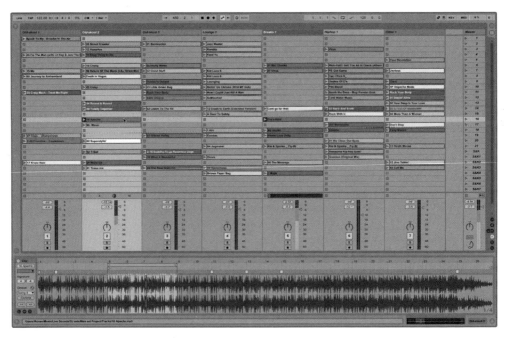

**Above:** This live Set is laid out by style, with some Scenes loosely used to facilitate easy triggering of full songs and looped sections that layer well.

## Setting Up a Cue Output

In the next section, we'll look at cueing, for which you'll need to set up a cue mix output from your audio interface. Assign the headphone output to its own bus in your interface's mixer application, then select that output in the Master Track's Cue Out menu. We'll come back to this shortly.

# PERFORMING YOUR DJ SET

Time to get that crowd moving!

## Triggering Clips and Scenes

If your clips are all correctly warped, no matter what you do – including changing tempo – everything will always stay in time. Playback of launched clips waits for the next time division

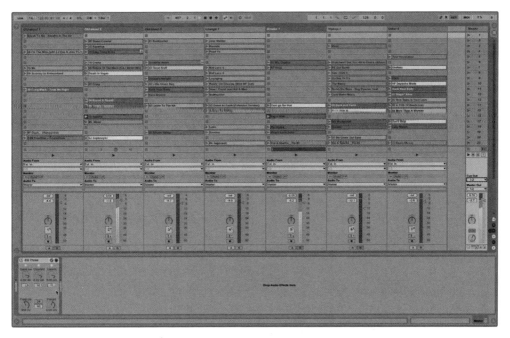

**Above:** Assign QWERTY keys to mixer buttons, device controls and clip slots in Key Map Mode.

set in the launch Quantization menu
(for which 1 Bar is generally the best
option), making it easy to mix between
songs, DJ-style, using the mixer controls
and Crossfader (see page 116). Press
Cmd/Ctrl+K to enter Key Map Mode,
in which selecting a clip slot or button
(Track Activators and Solo/Cues, and three
Crossfader positions, most pertinently)
and pressing a key on your QWERTY
keyboard assigns that key to launch the
slot or toggle the button.

## Hot Tip

Set the loop brace to loop
a short passage (the main beat,
say) within a song to have it roll
along under songs playing on
other tracks – a great tactic for
beat reinforcement and
rhythmic continuity
between songs.

## Cueing

1. The cue mix is a secondary audio bus that feeds a discrete signal to your headphones (heard only by you) separate from that going to the main mix (heard by the audience), for cueing up the next song to be played, setting up loops within songs prior to dropping them into the mix, tweaking effects, and any other situation in which you need to monitor a song without the audience hearing it.

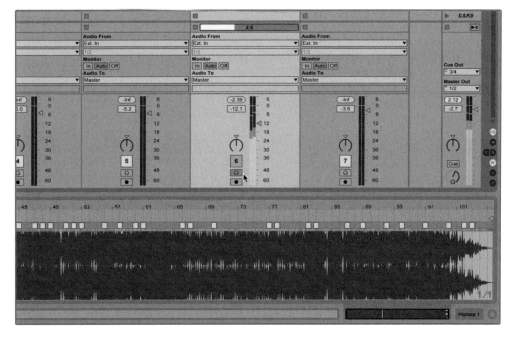

**Above:** Click the headphones buttons to route tracks to your headphones for 'silent' monitoring.

2. Click the Master Track Solo/Cue button to switch the Track Solo buttons to Cue buttons, then click a Cue button to route that track to your headphones. The Track Activator still determines whether or not the track is present in the main output, though, so make sure it's off if you don't want the audience to hear the clip when it's launched!

## Using the Crossfader

Click the Show/Hide Crossfader Section button (it looks like an X) to reveal the Crossfader and its associated controls. The Crossfader appears as a horizontal slider at the bottom of the Master Track, and clicking the A or B button under a track assigns it to its left- (A) or right- (B) hand side. Move the Crossfader left and right using the mouse, an assigned MIDI controller or three QWERTY keys (*see* page 113–14) to smoothly crossfade between A- and B-assigned tracks, just as you would with a DJ mixer and a pair of turntables. Tracks not assigned to A or B are unaffected.

**Hot Tip**

Right-click the Crossfader to select one of seven response curves.

**Below:** Mix between two or more tracks with the Crossfader.

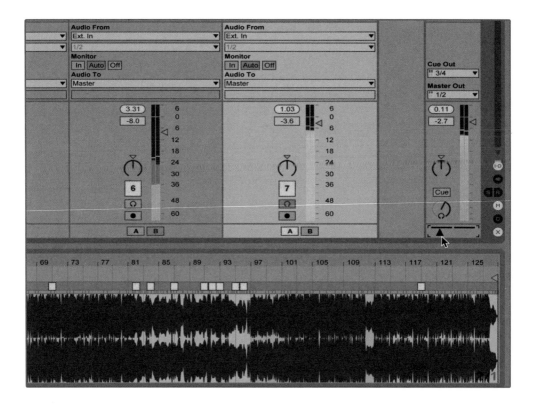

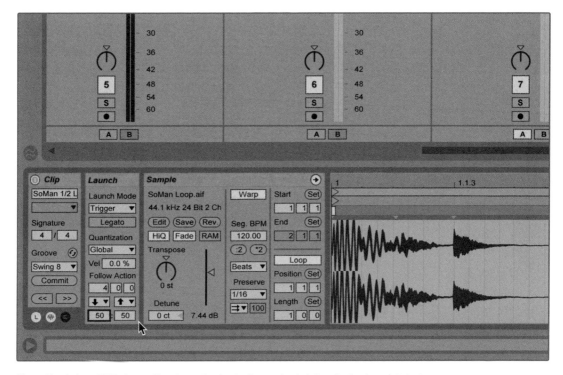

**Above:** This clip has a 50/50 chance of launching either the clip above or the clip below after four bars of playback.

## Follow Actions

Live's Follow Actions is a powerful system for automatically launching clips on the same track. It can be used to cycle through loops, create variations and more, in planned or random order.

The controls are found at the bottom of the Clip View's Launch box. Select one or two possible Follow Actions in the Follow Action A and B menus, and balance the probabilities of either one happening at the end of the time period set in the three fields immediately above (bars, beats, 16ths). The list of Follow Actions comprises Stop, Play Again, Previous/Next (play the previous or next clip), First/Last (play top/bottom clip), and Any (play any clip, including the current one or not).

## Applying DJ-Style Effects

Load the Master Track of your DJ Set with Live's EQ Three (emulating a DJ mixer EQ, complete with kill switches), and perhaps a handful of spot effects – reverb, delay and flanger, for example. Assign selected device parameters to a MIDI controller and QWERTY keys for hands-on tweaking – bypass buttons, kill switches, filter cutoff, reverb mix, etc. – and use them to spice up transitions between tracks, and create build and drops.

## Recording the Gig

Activate the Record button in Live's Control Bar before you start performing your DJ Set to have every move you make – from launching clips and crossfading to effects processing and tempo changes – captured in the Arrangement View, where you can edit and finesse it into the perfect mix, ready for export as a stereo WAV or AIFF.

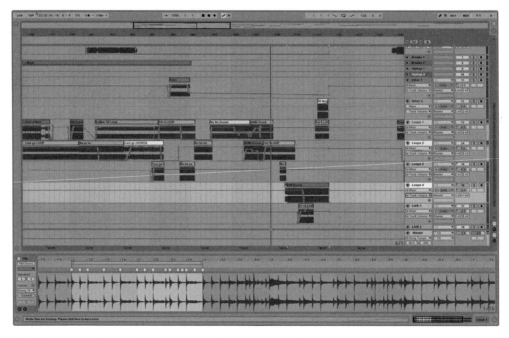

**Above:** Record your Session View DJ Set from start to finish in the Arrangement View.

# PERFORMING LIVE WITH LIVE

**Whether you use it as a multilayered instrument rack, a live looping rig or the central performance and recording hub for an entire band, Ableton Live is geared up for onstage antics of all kinds.**

## PLUGGING IN

If you're employing Live for one-person usage as a playable rack of virtual instruments, you should be good to go with just a basic audio interface and a suitable USB MIDI controller. If more than one person will be triggering MIDI instruments, you may need to invest in a USB hub to hook up the requisite number of controllers. If you're going to be processing and recording any number of external instruments (guitars, synths, etc.) and microphones, a fast (Thunderbolt, ideally), high-quality audio interface will be required, with enough inputs to plug them all in and perhaps enough outputs to feed monitor mixes to all concerned if you're not using stage wedges. Live monitor mixing is a subject beyond the scope of this book, but there's plenty of information and buying advice online. If money's tight, a simple headphone splitter will suffice, supplying a single monitor mix to everyone.

**Above:** If you're putting Live at the heart of your band's live act, monitoring is something you'll have to consider (Presonus HP4 Headphone Amp shown here).

# PERFORMING YOUR LIVE SET

There are many ways in which Live can be used onstage, so let's look at the main ones.

## Loops and Backing Tracks

Live can serve up loops and full tracks as the backing music for buskers, vocal groups, etc. If the backings are your own compositions,

### Hot Tip

To have Live's transport automatically follow the tempi of your backing tracks (for metronome accompaniment in mid-song solo sections, say), activate Warp on each one and incorporate its tempo into the Scene in which it lies. Launching a Scene instantly sets the project tempo to match.

**Below:** We've named the Scenes holding our six backing tracks with their BPMs included, so that Live's project tempo will change accordingly as each Scene is launched.

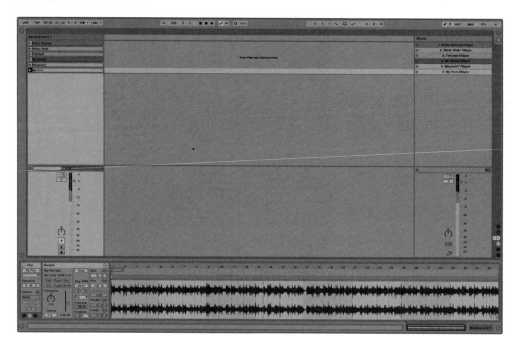

bounce them down as stereo mixes
rather than run them in 'project'
form, as this not only ensures
stability but also means you can
run a whole gig's worth of them in
a single Set. If you're working with
layered loops, lay out a Session View
Scene for each song and fire at will.
For full-length backing tracks, place
each one, unwarped and unlooped,
in its own clip slot on a single track.

## Playing Virtual Instruments Live

Live is renowned for its stability, making it a great option for hosting virtual instruments in a
live performance setting, with or without accompanying loops and backing tracks (*see* previous
page). Set up a track for each song in your live set – and, indeed, Live Set – containing the
devices and plugins required, assign a few Macros to simplify parameter adjustment, plug
in your MIDI controller(s) and switch between tracks during the gig. Apart from possible
stability issues with specific plugins (test them thoroughly first!), the only significant snag
you might encounter is latency – that is, the delay between pressing a key on your MIDI

**Above**: With a super-fast Thunderbolt audio interface, latency won't be a problem (ZOOM's TAC-8 Thunderbolt Audio Converter shown here).

keyboard or hitting a drum pad and the virtual instrument sounding. With a high-quality USB or Thunderbolt audio interface, though, you should be able to get this below the generally accepted playability threshold of 10 milliseconds.

**Above:** Run your whole band through Live and you can apply effects, mix in virtual instruments and pre-prepared clips, and record the mix.

## Playing and Sampling Real Instruments Live

As well as virtual synths and samplers, Live can receive input from any number of guitars, microphones, hardware synths, etc., for multitrack recording of performances and real-time processing of instruments and vocals live on stage. The main technical considerations here are the audio interface and monitoring, as noted on page 119; and a metronomic click track will probably need to be deployed to keep everyone in time with Live's clock. Latency can be a problem when running live audio input through effects, but with a fast interface and sensible effects choices, this should be more than manageable. If you can keep the effects to Ableton's own devices, you'll minimize any risk with regard to stability.

With the band plugged in, set up device chains for each instrument, perhaps with each player operating theirs using a dedicated MIDI controller. Use Scenes to trigger incidental loops, change tempo for click tracks and effects synchronization, etc.; and record new clips on the fly without interrupting playback. Clips can be recorded into individual clip slots, or into all armed slots in the selected scene using the Session Record button (*see* next page).

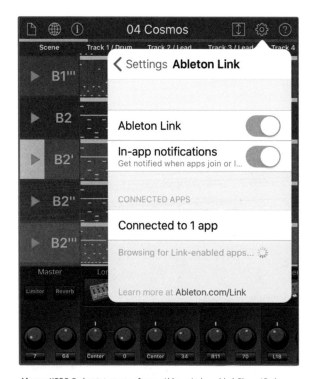

**Above:** KORG Gadget is just one of many Ableton Link-enabled iPhone/iPad apps.

Hit the Arrangement Record button and the audio and MIDI received by armed tracks will be recorded into the Arrangement View, along with all parameter automation, clip launches and Scene changes – just like recording your band in the studio.

## Live Looping

One of the Session View's big selling points is its ability to record then seamlessly begin playback of perfectly sized new clips while playing back any number of existing clips. Using this remarkable feature, you can, for example, grab a guitar riff as it happens in the heat of the moment, play it back as a loop and have the same guitarist immediately play a solo over the top of it. With the track or tracks armed for recording, hit the Record button on a clip slot, or the Session Record button to start recording at the next Quantization division (1 Bar, most likely), then click it again to switch from recording to playback. This also works for MIDI clips, of course.

---

### Hot Tip

Ableton Link is a wireless synchronization protocol supported by an increasing number of iOS music apps. Use it to incorporate iPhone and iPad instruments into your live shows, and sync multiple instances of Live across laptops.

The loop brace within a clip can be resized and moved in real time without breaking playback too. The Loop section of the Sample/Notes box in the Clip View contains MIDI-assignable fields and MIDI/QWERTY-assignable Set buttons for changing the position and length of the brace. Click the Set buttons to set the loop Start or End point to the nearest Quantization division to the current playback position. Playback always stays locked to the relative bar position, so you can mess around with the loop brace as much as you like without skipping a beat – as long as Quantize is on!

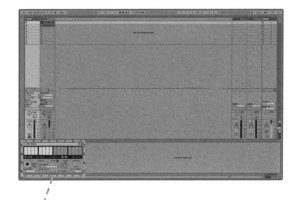

Live also includes the superb Looper device, which works just like the guitar pedal of the same name.

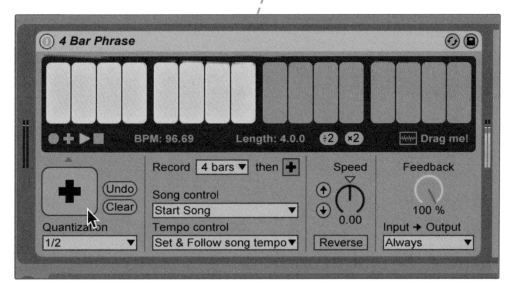

**Above**: Live's Looper device is the software equivalent of the looper pedals currently so in vogue with street musicians – it's awesome!

# USEFUL WEBSITES AND FURTHER READING

## WEBSITES

**www.ableton.com/en/help**
Ableton's official website offering help
on all products and answers to FAQs.

**www.abletunes.com**
Launched with the aim of creating quality Ableton
Live projects for novice producers who want to
learn music production with Ableton Live.

**www.gearslutz.com**
Forum for sharing information about audio
recording, production techniques and the
latest softwares.

**www.musicradar.com**
Find expert reviews of music equipment, tips,
projects and video tutorials on new software.

**www.musictech.net**
Website dedicated to the latest trends,
techniques, gear and software in the industry,
featuring tutorials, reviews and news updates.

**www.soundonsound.com**
A website with the latest music news and sound
techniques which also features a forum space.

**www.support.serato.com**
A quick start guide on how to use Ableton Live.

**https://tutsplus.com**
Tutorials, videos, online courses and articles to
help you learn all manner of skills – type in 'DAW'
or 'Ableton Live' and see what comes up.

## FURTHER READING

Bess, Josh, *Ableton Grooves: Programming Basic
and Advanced Grooves with Ableton Live*, Hal
Leonard Publishing Corporation, 2013

Katz, B., *Mastering Audio: The Art and the
Science*,  Focal Press, 2014

Macdonald, Ronan, *Mixing for Computer
Musicians (Everyday Guides, Made Easy)*,
Flame Tree Publishing, 2015

Marguiles, Jon, *Ableton Live 9 Power!
The Comprehensive Guide*, Delmar Cengage
Learning, 2013

Perrine, Jake, *Sound Design, Mixing and
Mastering with Ableton Live 9*, Hal Leonard
Publishing Corporation, 2014

Perrine, Jake, *Producing Music with Ableton Live
9*, Hal Leonard Publishing Corporation, 2014

Reiss, J.D., *Audio Effects: Theory, Implementation
and Application*, CRC Press, 2014

Robinson, Keith, *Ableton Live 9: Create, Produce,
Perform*, Focal Press, 2014

Strong, Jeff, *Home Recording for Musicians
for Dummies*, John Wiley & Sons, 2014

# INDEX